ALSO BY BETTE MIDLER

The Saga of Baby Divine

A VIEW FROM A BROAD

❀

·B·E·T·T·E·
·M·I·D·L·E·R·

Photography by Sean Russell

SIMON & SCHUSTER

New York   London   Toronto   Sydney   New Delhi

Special thanks to Jerry Blatt

Simon & Schuster
1230 Avenue of the Americas
New York, NY 10020

First Simon & Schuster hardcover edition April 2014

SIMON & SCHUSTER and colophon are registered trademarks of Simon & Schuster, Inc.

For information about special discounts for bulk purchases, please contact
Simon & Schuster Special Sales at 1-866-506-1949 or business@simonandschuster.com

The Simon & Schuster Speakers Bureau can bring authors to your live event.
For more information or to book an event contact the Simon & Schuster Speakers
Bureau at 1-866-248-3049 or visit our website at www.simonspeakers.com.

Interior design by Joel Avriom

Manufactured in the United States of America

10 9 8 7 6 5 4 3 2

The Library of Congress Cataloging in Publication Data:

Midler, Bette.
A view from a broad.
1. Midler, Bette. 2. Singers—United Staes—Biography. I. Title.
ML420.M43A3784'.092'479-23656

ISBN 978-1-4767-7355-1
ISBN 978-1-4767-7440-4 (ebook)

Grateful acknowledgment is given for permission to quote from "The Birds" by Neil
Young. Copyright © 1970 by Cotillion Music, Inc., and Broken Arrow Music Publishing
Co. All rights reserved.

Grateful acknowledgment is also made to Fifth Floor Music, Inc., for permission to quote
lyrics from "Shiver Me Timbers" by Tom Waits. Copyright © 1974 by Fifth Floor Music,
Inc. All rights reserved.

For my mother
· RUTH SCHINDEL MIDLER ·
With Everlasting Love

Fly away,
Fly away,
I'll close my eyes
And I will fly away . . .

—NEIL YOUNG

TO FRANK LLOYD & WILBUR WRIGHT WITHOUT WHOM THIS BOOK 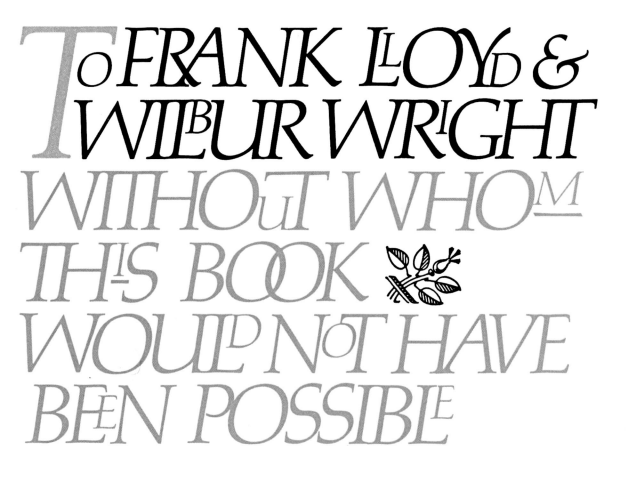 WOULD NOT HAVE BEEN POSSIBLE

CONTENTS

XVII   **INTRODUCTION**

1   **IT BEGINS**

17   **CLOUDS ON THE HORIZON**

33   **DEATH BY RELISH**

On the Distressing Aspects of Being Interviewed

47   **OPENING NIGHT LONDON**

The Mouth of the Thames

65   **CHOPPED HERRING**

The Continental Divine

81   **THIGHS AND WHISPERS**

95   **SOMEWHERE IN THE NORTH OF FRANCE**

Rantings of a Manic Mermaid

111   **AT THE GERMAN BORDER**

121   **CONFESSIONS OF A HASH EATER**

130   **THE RIVER OF KINGS**

136   **AN AMERICAN IN SYDNEY**

142   **HOT WIND**

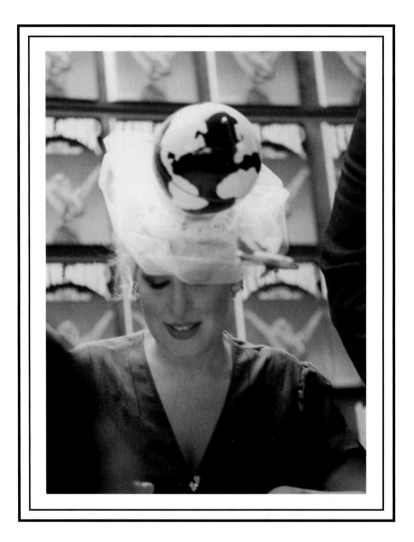

L

ong, long ago, around 1980, through a veil of hot, briny tears, I seem to recall that I toured the world with my show, for the first time, and lived to tell. The book you hold in your hands was the "confaction" that came out of that tour. I was thirty-five years old, cute as a button and excited beyond belief. I was going to see the world, and the world was going to see me. "I knew so little of the world: Slander, not geography, had always been my strong suit" . . . and there was more than a grain of truth in that. I was clueless. My international travel was limited to an earlier trip to Paris, where I was surrounded by schoolchildren who made fun of my shoes.

We were a motley crew; a quarrelsome band that murdered the time; three libidinous girl singers; and many, many attractive soundmen, stagehands, road managers, drivers, and fans. It was a powder keg, to put it mildly. Add in new and various faces and races that wanted to be our best friends every third day, new drugs to try and new bars to visit, and you can imagine how hard it was to keep chaos at bay.

One of the things that surprised me most was that the world knew me! And they seemed to love me and showered me with affection at every stop: bouquets, gifts, letters, notes, telegrams, confetti, invitations and standing ovations. It was a whirlwind, a mob scene; I was at the center of it and it was hard to separate the best intentions from the worst.

And the shows were great; some of the best of my life.

In those days, if I had even the germ of an idea, someone would move heaven and earth to make it happen. I am a reader, and have been my whole life. I love books, and love all the romance associated with them. The bindings! The illustrations by N. C. Wyeth, Maxfield

Parrish, Jesse Wilcox Smith, et al. . . . The dreadful lives that everyone led, being paid by the word, too tragic. Those green eyeshades! Fabulous! I even adore editors: How marvelous to be squirrelled away in some dank corner spinning literary dross into gold!

I had decided I wanted to do a book before we started rehearsals, and lo and behold, the publishers were lined up in droves. What clout I had in those days! My best friend, Jerry, and his boyfriend, Sean (not his real name, which was Wesley—don't ask), searched maps and guidebooks to decide where we could shoot pictures to accompany whatever was to come. We did many by-the-seat-of-our-pants photo shoots when abroad, like the Penguin Parade in Australia, and though most of the photos never made the book, I remember many of the charming, out-of-the-way places we found; the taxidermy store in Paris, the monastery outside Munich, musty old London bookstalls.

Things happened. There were fistfights, fires, drugs, accidents, arrests, screaming matches, phones thrown at old friends and way too much press to face, day after day, bruises and all. It was not a pretty picture. Couples paired off, or didn't . . . one couple married after that tour is still married; a driver I adored got sick and died not long after we left.

The challenge was to make it funny, and when I finally got home, I found that a lot of it was. But a lot of it wasn't, and I finally had to face it. After this tour, I knew that certain things were not for me, and that I had to make a choice. Could I continue to make a joyful noise when I was angry, ill and hungover? Some can, but I couldn't. My manager, Aaron Russo, and I broke up after a series of violent fights, and I had to live without the kind of support I had had for more than ten years. It's not an exaggeration to say that that tour changed my life.

So this book was a kind of last hurrah. When I read it, I hear a disarmingly younger, sweeter voice, a character I adore, but whom I don't hear from much anymore. I loved her, and mourn her from time to time, like Márgarét on page 129.

By 1980, the '60s were finally over. The cloud of HIV/AIDS was about to descend on the blue-sky world I lived in, taking with it a whole generation of artists, performers and friends, including Jerry and Sean. I am not sure that this little confection captures a whole time, but I think it's an accurate picture of the spirit and tone of what I was doing in those days. I hope it holds up, and that you find your best younger self in it, as I do.

—*Bette Midler*
October 2013

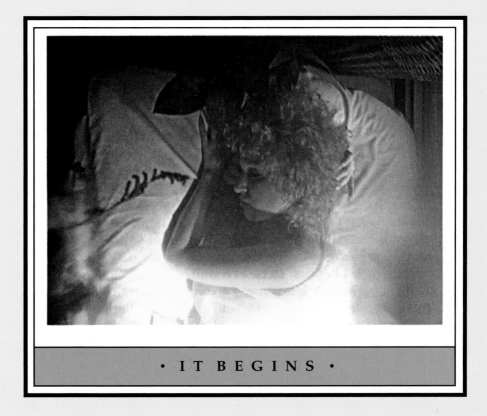

· I T B E G I N S ·

*"I knew so little of the world, really.
Slander, not geography, had always
been my strongest suit."*

I will never forget it! Only moments before I found out that a world tour was being planned for me, I was exactly where I most like to be—flat on my back on my lovely redwood deck, overlooking the glorious, ever-changing moods of the Santa Ana Freeway. I was truly at peace. And I was truly a mess, having just forged my way through the potentially crippling round of severe calisthenics I dutifully perform every evening of the year. Well, almost every evening. If I happen to be at home.

Actually, I shouldn't belittle my exercises so by calling them calisthenics when they are, in fact, a unique distillation of semiclassical semidance movements designed specifically with my very own body proportions in mind by the well-known physiotherapist Dr. D . . ., who, though only thirty-two, and having no congenital defects worth mentioning, can barely stand up straight. This apparent conflict between what Dr. D . . . claims his program can do for the human physique and what it has actually done to his seems to have had no effect whatsoever on his Hollywood following. In fact, there is a small, shrill clique of high-profile Hollywoodites who claim that Dr. D . . . is the very Messiah of Serious Body Building. Not body building, of course, in the sense of that atavistic desire and/or need to lift heavy metal to face level, but body building in the more mystical sense: training that complex jumble of tissue and electrochemical reactions to become an instrument totally subservient to one's will, ready to meet life's every challenge no matter how sordid or bizarre.

Little did I know what challenges I was to face—or how soon —when sprawled out and panting on my deck I suddenly realized that the loud knocking I was hearing was not the frenzied beating of my heart but someone beating frantically at my door. As I ran, still dazed and blinded by sweat, to answer the insistent call, I took, quite literally a turn for the worse and ricocheted off a mirrored wall colliding, *tete a tete*, with the life-size statue of the Bloated Buddha I'd unearthed just recently at a swap meet in Anaheim. I had placed the porcelain wonder in my vestibule in the fervid hope that from it might emanate a flow of tranquillity to counteract the general uproar of my household. Now the statue lay shattered in a thousand pieces. *Not* a good omen.

As my maid, the unflappable Aretha, began to vacuum around me, I made one or two unsuccessful attempts to rise out of the debris. I was just about to despair of ever walking again when suddenly the knocking stopped and I heard a key turn in the lock. Only one person had a key to my house. I wish I could say it was a lover or even a close and dear friend. But no, it was my manager, a man of direct action and some girth, whose emotional response to any given event was generally the exact opposite of mine. One look at his smiling face and I *knew* I was in trouble.

> *"Little did I know what challenges I was to face—or how soon . . ."*

"Here," I said holding up one of my ex-Buddha's ears, "it's yours. I've decided to become a Taoist. I go into retreat tomorrow."

Without even the slightest acknowledgment of my offering or my bruises, the heartless man pulled a thick purple folder from his pocket and threw it a few feet from where I lay collapsed on the floor.

"Read that!" he commanded in a tone most often used by major generals and some minor household gods.

Brushing away the hair from my eyes and the evil thoughts from my heart, I crawled through the litter of broken mirror and porcelain limbs towards the mysterious folder.

"Itinerary!" he said proudly as I retrieved it.

"You what?" I began, then stopped short, dumbstruck, as I stared open-mouthed at the very first page:

BETTE MIDLER WORLD TOUR

Opening Dates—Number of Performances

Sept. 11—Seattle (three nights)
17—London (five nights)
27—Brighton (one night)
30—Gothenburg (one night)

Oct. 1—Stockholm (one night, two shows)
2—Copenhagen (one night)
3—Lund (one night)
6—Hamburg (one night)
7—Frankfurt (one night)
8—Munich (one night)
10—Paris (two nights)
13—The Hague (one night)
14—Antwerp (one night)
16—Amsterdam (two nights, four shows)
25—Sydney (five nights)

Nov. 1—Melbourne (one night)
4—Perth (one night)
7—Adelaide (one night)
9—Brisbane (one night)
12—Sydney (three nights)
17—Honolulu?

I couldn't believe my eyes! It was truly an astonishment of nations. I looked up at my manager, then back to the purple folder, flipping frantically towards the middle, where the entire project was fully outlined in all its fearsome detail:

October 17

8 A.M.	Bette, Band, Harlettes check out of hotel in Amsterdam.
9 A.M.	Train or limo to The Hague. All check into The Hague Hilton. Free lunch served to all in the Tulip Lounge, except Miss Midler, who goes directly to press conference.
4 P.M.	Sound check.
7 P.M.	Light food served for cast & crew. Miss Midler, at manager's request, will not receive food or drink until after the show.
8 P.M.	Curtain.

October 18

7 A.M.	Meet in lobby. Check out. Remember, you pay your incidentals. Bette: All calls to Peter will be charged to your room.
8 A.M.	Entire company train or limo to Antwerp. You must clear Customs yourself. Please! BE CAREFUL. Remember, our motto on this trip: No lust, no dust, no bust. And try to get rid of your change. New currency this afternoon.
4 P.M.	Sound check. (May be later if elephants have not vacated hall by 3.)

7 P.M.	Cast & crew to band room for dinner. Miss Midler to dressing room for candid photo session.
8 P.M.	Curtain.
	NOTE: This venue has no curtain. This stage is at floor level and less than 14 feet wide. Lighting and sound facilities are minimal. Certain adjustments may have to be made. BE PREPARED.
12 P.M.	Special tour of Antwerp night spots leaves from hotel lobby.
12:15 A.M.	Return to hotel.
12:20 A.M.	Lights out.

October 19

8 A.M.	Entire company drive from Antwerp to Brussels airport. Clear Customs. Change money into Marks. Pray the poor dollar isn't out for the count.
11:15 A.M.	Leave Brussels.
12:25 P.M.	Arrive Frankfurt. Clear Customs.
1 P.M.	Lunch for troupe in Beethoven Lounge. Miss Midler to beauty parlor for perm.
4 P.M.	Sound check.
7 P.M.	The promoters have arranged for a light dinner, but be careful. Some have complained of aftereffects from local food here. Lomotil available at light booth. Miss Midler to basement to meet local dignitaries.
8:15 P.M.	Curtain.

I didn't know what to do, what to say. Once again a questionable consortium of managers, agents, lawyers and record promoters had concocted a plan for me that would force me out of my cozy existence and into a maelstrom of madness. Once again, just when visions of breakfast in bed and phones off the hook promised to become reality, I would have to go back to work.

It wasn't that I didn't *want* to work. I enjoy working, tremendously. But I had just finished making my very first movie, *The Rose*—if you are kind enough not to consider my celluloid interpretation of Mary, Mother of God, which I did for seventy bucks one afternoon in Detroit to pay for a phone call to my mom in Honolulu—and the experience had left me exhilarated but worn to a shadow. There were so many new things to contend with—like getting up at 6 A.M., getting to know what a gaffer was and, most important, getting thin. Of course, there were some initial difficulties when the director first told me the disappointing news that if the film was to have any semblance of reality at all there would have to be moments when other people were onscreen at the same time I was. My despair over this turn of events was, however, somewhat ameliorated by the fact that the person

I most often had to share the screen with turned out to be Alan Bates, whose unforgettable fig-sucking scene in *Women in Love* literally changed my life. Actually, I found I liked film acting quite a lot, although not half as much as I liked my trailer, which is exactly the kind of home I hope to have someday.

So it was not just having to work again that bothered me. I was pained to think that I would have to leave my beloved Los Angeles, with all its attendant glory, and travel to places whose names I had never even heard and, upon hearing, could scarcely pronounce. I knew so little of the world, really. Slander, not geography, has always been my strongest suit. The closest thing

> *". . . I liked film acting quite a lot, although not half as much as I liked my trailer . . ."*

I had ever had to a foreign experience was Ahmet Ertegun, record executive and Turk. Oh, I was truly in a dither.

With a flair for the dramatic that annoys almost everyone around me, I flung open an exquisite set of priceless French doors and looked out at the Greater Los Angeles Basin, twitching below me in the dying August sun. On the other side of the Freeway, hundreds of hummingbirds were gathering in the twilight, preparing to ravage my bougainvillea. How could I leave this throbbing center of vitality and delight, this modern Athens, this garbanzo in the salad of human achievement, and travel to places where the plumbing was uncertain and where there might not be even one Chinese restaurant?

My exercises, which usually have such a calming effect on me, failed me completely, and I flew into a tantrum of panic and despair so titanic that even my longtime companion and wardrobe mistress, the very proper Miss Frann Frank, born, bred and even beaned once in Boston at a Red Sox game, became fearful —not so much for me as for her new issue of *Watchtower*, which I had ripped out of her hands and was about to gobble down, admonitions and all.

Fortunately, good sense and a slap across the face were to prevail. In fact, after several hours of pouting and pacing and just the teeniest nip or two of Courvoisier, going around the world began to have its appeal.

First of all, my manager's incessant yapping in my ear about International Launching Pads and Smart Career Moves made me so furious I would have gone anywhere to get away from him. Even Lund. Wherever that was.

Secondly, I felt that my mind, unquenchable in its thirst for cultural enrichment and cheap thrills, might benefit from such a world-girdling juggernaut. So, in fact, might my jugs, which, despite my strict adherence to Dr. D . . .'s routines, were beginning to turn to mush in the soft California air.

But beyond all that, the fact was that I had always had a burning desire to see the world. When I was a little girl in Honolulu, all my friends and neighbors, everyone I went to school with, had their roots in some romantic place or other—China, Japan, Malaya, the Philippines—while my folks hailed from New Jersey. My father had moved out to Hawaii during the Depression, not so much to find work as to find a proper setting for my mother, whom he always thought too beautiful and delicate for prosaic Passaic.

But growing up in Paradise was difficult for me. I always felt so boring next to the people around me, so colorless. In such exotic company, I was a hopelessly mundane transplant, a common, worthless dandelion lost in a garden of orchids. Just hearing my teacher call out the names of the kids in my class— Akamatsu, Yick Lung, Tuituila, In'nopu—would set me off on the wildest kind of daydreaming.

As I looked through the purple folder again, those old luscious waves of Longing and Romance crested and crashed upon the shores of my very being. For a moment, I felt ten again, and I realized that even though I had never done it before, going around the world would be, for me, a kind of a sentimental journey. And the only thing I put above Sentiment is Revenge.

And so it was that as the sun set somewhere in the middle of August, I gathered up the broken shards of my Buddha and my life and committed myself. The Bette Midler World Tour was on. I would pick up the gauntlet my manager had thrown down and touch the whole earth with my Divinity.

Dizzy with exhilaration and dread, I took my favorite Paper Mate in hand and began to do what I always do in a situation that demands bold and forthright action: I made lists.

In the Next
Ten Minutes
I Must:

M E

3. Have passport photos retouched

1. Learn to decline in SEVEN tongues

By air mail
Par avion

By air mail
Par avion

(2.) Buy a globe. Study it. Try to find Lund.

(4.) Have a chat with musician union. (SPEAK SLOWLY Ascertain minimum wage for all countries on itinerary.

* 5. Keep this information Secret.

(6.) Clean up garage for Band Auditions.

7.
If still of sound mind, call: Drugstore, Doctor, Dentist, Chiropractor, Speech Therapist, PETER , Masseur, Rehearsal Hall, FAmily, Doctor D., Guard Dog Trainer Locksmith, Insurance Agent, Pacific Tel., Pacific Gas & Electric, Milkman, Post office, Gardener, Druggist, Pool Person, Service, shoemaker, Optometrist, GURU, Grocer, Stock Broker, Astrologer

M O

8.)

Phone

Choreographer

(Try to be

pleasant.)

9.

Interview:
Soundman,
Lighting man,
Costumer,
Set Designer,
Hairdresser,
Road Manager,
Makeup man,
Prop man.
(Plead poverty
to one + all.)

10.

Remain

Tranquil

	THOUGHTS TO BE AVOIDED
1.	They won't understand a word I say.
2.	They WILL UNDERSTAND and take offense.
3.	They won't understand BUT will take offense anyway.
4.	They will purchase hard candies and hurl them at the stage.
5.	I will be invited to an Oktoberfest, where I will be forced to stomp the grapes and cut the cheese.
6.	ONLY raw herring will be served wherever I go.
7.	Even my use of the knife and fork will brand me a stranger.
8.	I will stand in tears amid the alien corn.
9	I will come home in failure and financial ruin.
10.	I DESERVE WHATEVER I GET.

"How I uncover talent . . ."

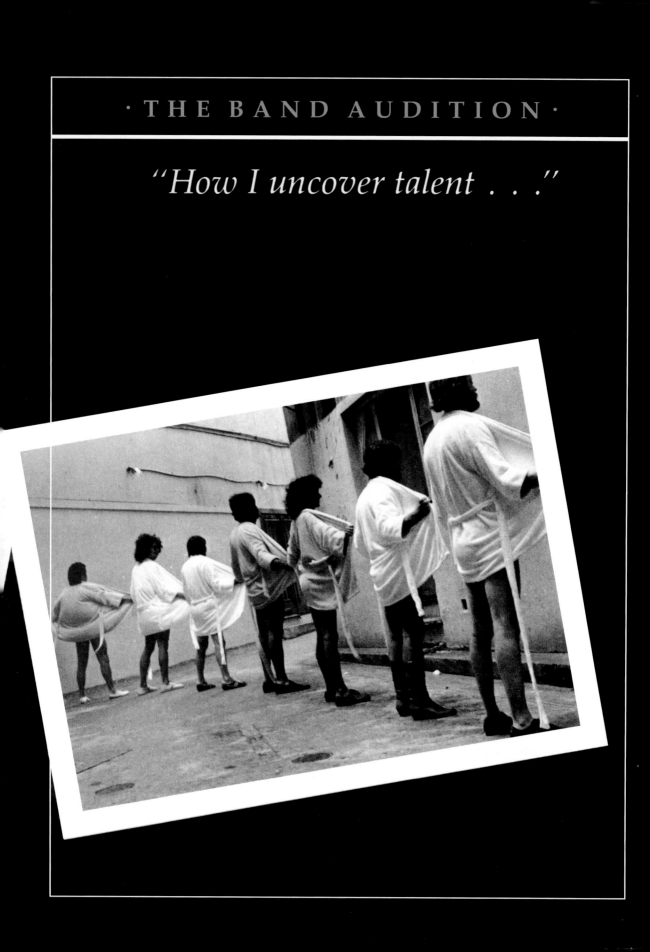

For the Reader's Edification: Often I am asked how I have managed so consistently to surround myself with people of the highest creative caliber. I offer the following application as but one of the ways in which I uncover talent and excellence that might otherwise lie fallow in the fetid hog wallow that we call the field of entertainment.

BAND APPLICATION

Name _____

Alias _____

Ht._____ Wt._____ Color of eyes_____

Favorite Female Performer _____

Please answer the following questions:

Will you work for scale? Yes_____ No _____

When was the last time you were in jail?_____

Offense and length of term _____

Have you ever physically attacked a performer under whose employ you were at the

time? Yes_____ No _____

If yes, was it: Onstage_____ Offstage_____ In the privacy of her home _____

Do you take drugs? Yes_____ No_____ Not sure _____

Can you arrange for your own supply? Yes_____ No_____ On occasion _____

Can you arrange for mine? Yes_____ No_____ On occasion_____

List your major contacts in a. Europe_____ b. Australia_____ c. Seattle _____

Do you consider your sex drive to be:

Normal_____ Above normal_____ Monklike_____

In a no-sex situation do you: Play well_____Play badly _____

Quit_____

Have you been able to read this application by yourself? Yes____No ____Sort of ____

THE WINNERS!

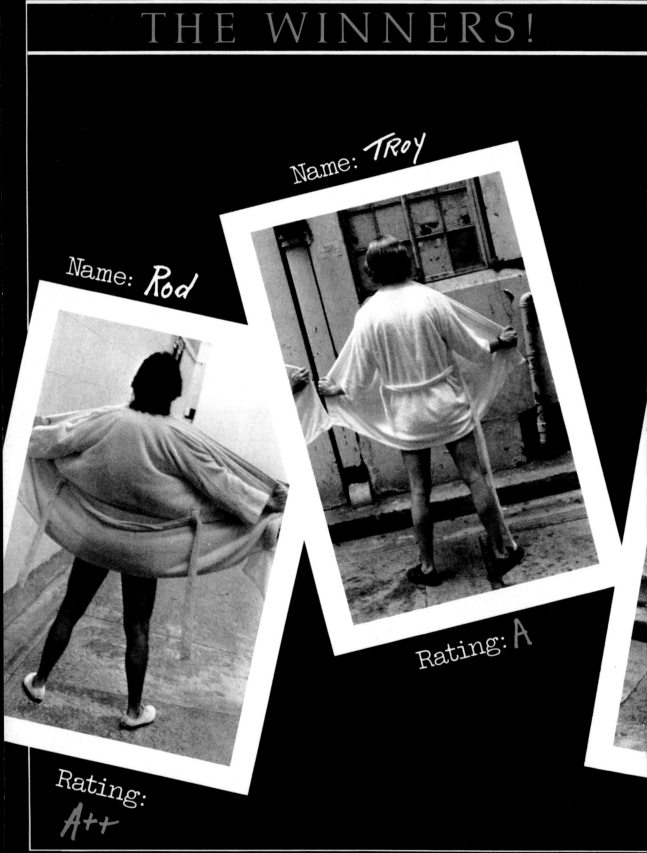

Name: Rod

Name: TROY

Rating: A

Rating: A++

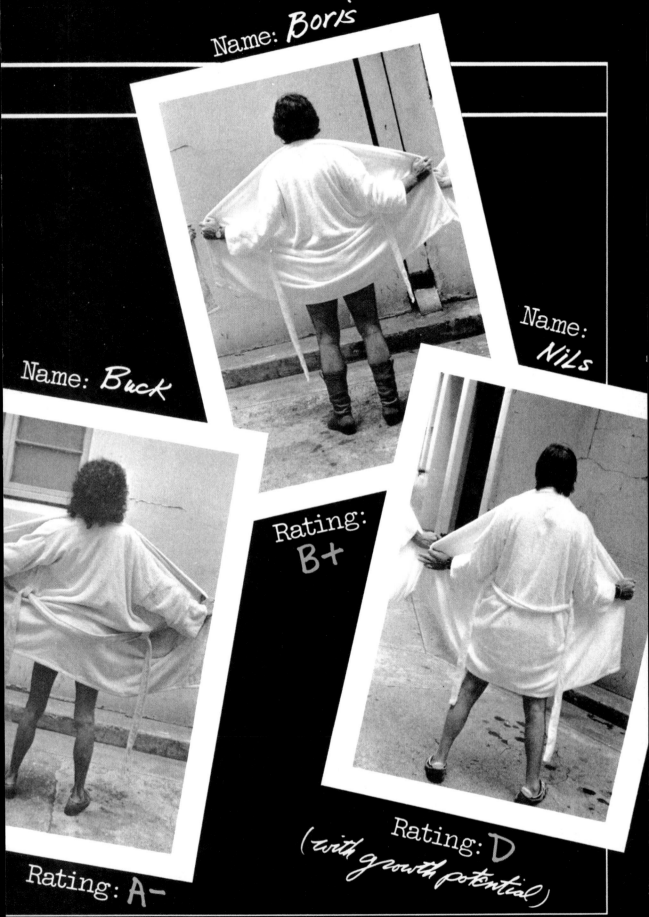

Name: *Boris*

Name: *Nils*

Name: *Buck*

Rating:
B+

Rating: D
(with growth potential)

Rating: A-

· CLOUDS ON THE HORIZON ·

"The World is my shoehorn;
I shall not shlep . . ."

DIVINE REVELATIONS, Chapter 8: Verse 6

There is no rest for the weary. No sooner had the gathering-of-the-forces been accomplished than I had to throw myself into the excruciating process of creating a show that would do two things at one and the same time: a) bring the world to its knees, and b) fit into a footlocker.

Unfortunately, these two objectives were not easily reconciled, and this was causing a severe change in my ordinarily placid, even decorous behavior.

For days on end, I would hardly speak, and when I did only the vilest sort of gibberish would spout forth. I became morose and fat. Unapproachable, except when eating—and then only by waiters. I became, in short, a walking fountain of misery and despair. And not only were my metaphors mixed: my entire thinking process was deranged, and I found myself dwelling, in the *most* morbid fashion, on the very things I had vowed not to think about at all. Every day, for example, I'd get up and stare in total panic at the seven little phrase books hanging so cheerily from my bedpost.

You see, on stage, as in life, I talk *a lot*. In fact, random, rambling raillery makes up a rather large part of my act and I absolutely depend on it. People often say, "My, but the little vixen has a lot of energy," mostly because I never shut up. But chatter is a respite for me, like treading water after miles of the Australian crawl, and the water that keeps me afloat, the English language. What would I do in, let's say, Sweden? The few basic words I was gleaning from my phrase books hardly scratched the surface of my needs. I was, indeed, one scared piece of Divinity.

I began to have recurring nightmares. In one of them, the instant I hit the stage icicles formed on the proscenium arch; snow

> *"I was, indeed, one scared piece of Divinity."*

fell from the flies; and a thick layer of hoarfrost covered the faces of the crowd which lay stretched out before me like the Dead Sea. Frozen to the spot, I could neither sing nor speak nor even cry out as the entire audience rose up as one, pelted me with Eskimo Pies, and walked out.

Yes, I had terrible fears of what *might* happen, but they were as nothing when compared with what really *was* happening.

My new band was crumbling under the pressure of trying to learn a wildly eclectic score from music sheets written in wildly divergent keys, the gift of some sadistic copyist who, I had no doubt, was working for Helen Reddy. Guitar players came and went with a regularity my nerve-racked system could only envy.

My manager had blithely informed me that he would be coming along on the *entire* trip, and suddenly I understood why he had planned the trek in the first place. After all, the most exotic place the man had ever been to was Las Vegas.

My choreographer had, since I last worked with her, turned in her tutus and plunged into Punk. This time out, number after number emerged dripping with violence and hostility. Every day she would come into rehearsal, the tattered threads of what was left of her mental fabric trailing behind her. And there she would sit: back straight, head held high, barking out the steps of the day from her makeshift throne. "*Pas de bourée*, step step; *pas de bourée*, step step; *tour jeté*, step, turn; Katie rip off Linda's wig!"

We all worked as hard as we could to fulfill her vision, but it didn't make any difference how we stomped about. We tried to be up-to-the-minute, but it was no use. Invariably, she would sit there, occasionally raising her eyebrows, indicating, with weary little sighs she let escape now and then, that I should quit while I was ahead and cancel the tour before the rest of the world could plumb for itself the depths of my incompetence.

Still, for all her safety pins, alligator clips, and acute lack of enthusiasm, she *was* a wonderful choreographer, and I loved the way she perceived the world. Once she told me that she had seen Baryshnikov and Kirkland dance *Giselle*. I asked her how it was. "Oh, doll," she said, "I loved it, but they were *so* brilliant and *so* pompous I was afraid God would strike them down dead."

How Old Testament of her. Here was a woman who could surprise me. I liked that *and* the extension cords she wore around her neck in her quest for the true Punk pose. But, my dears, I could have used *some* encouragement.

My choreographer had turned in her tutus and plunged into punk.

Miss Frank, my dresser and confidante of so many years, was no help either. She would constantly hint—or outright tell me—that it was both foolish *and* dangerous to think I had something the entire world was panting for.

"Pride goeth before destruction, and a haughty spirit before a fall," she would intone while hemming up my skirt or pinning down my cleavage. "There's a punishment coming. That's for sure. I can feel it in my bones."

"That's polio, dear," I would tell the silly woman, but to no avail.

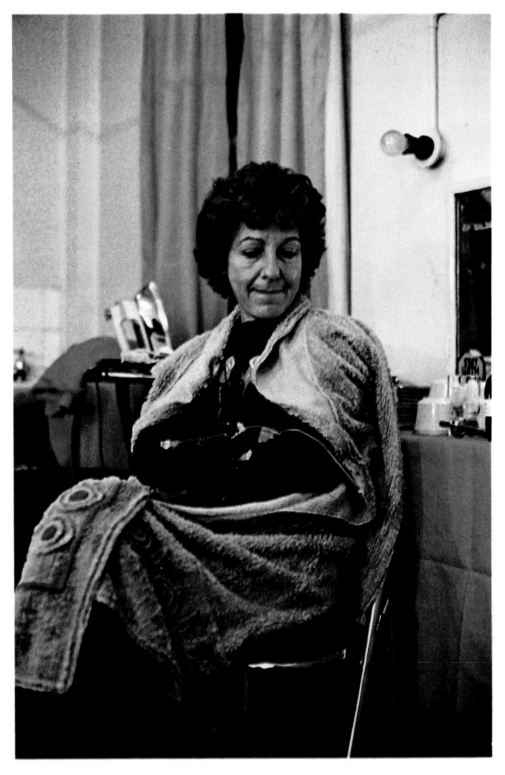

Miss Frank was no help either.

T H E
· H A R L E T T E S ·
My
**three favorite chotchkes
on the breakfront of life!**

Of course, I shouldn't have been surprised by Miss Frank's behavior. Miss Frank has always been, and I hope always will be, the very model of humility and moral rectitude. As, indeed, am I, although she does not think so. Being moral isn't what you *do*, I have often tried to tell her, it's what you *mean* to do. And, naturally, I always mean the best.

Miss Frank remains unconvinced of my virtue and in deep concern for my immortal soul. I'm sure the only reason she comes along with me on these monumental shleps is because she considers it her duty to save me from the perils that can befall a young woman of my station and bodily proportions. "The road!" Miss Frank proclaims each time we go on tour. "Why, it's the Devil's Walkway, and anyone who trods it is bound to Hula in Hell." Well, what can you do? She's *such* a good dresser. It must be all those steeples in Boston. But then again, who knows? Certainly not I. I know nothing, despite my avid thirst for knowledge and enlightenment. While others study, explore, experience, I go to fittings.

But be that as it may. In those early, dark days of rehearsal, only my new Harlettes—Katie, Franny and Linda—gave me comfort. From the very first moment I discovered them, selling their cherries at the Farmers' Market, they never let me down. I had to find new background singers for my Grand Tour, because my old ones had decided to find fame and fortune on their own. I was pissed, but not surprised. You know me: Bette Midler, brood hen to the stars—Barry Manilow, Melissa Manchester, the Platform Shoe. And actually, I adored my new threesome. When others turned their backs on this hapless Diva, my Harlettes did what they could to shore me up against the tidal waves of depression that threatened to engulf the vast, cold spaces of Rehearsal Hall 6. For not only were my girls fine singers and dancers, they also thought I was God.

Oh, those girls! My three favorite chotchkes on the breakfront of life! I'll never forget how they looked when I first saw them— so flushed, so filthy. But I knew, even then, that under those dirt-streaked, rouge-stained cheeks, there was Magic.

The shocking verbal abuse they hurled at me when I first approached them only made me more certain I was right. I could do so much with them, I thought. And *for* them. Duty was not the exclusive province of Miss Frank. I would be more than their employer, I would be their Benefactress. I would raise them out of the gutter, nourish their minds, their souls, be privy to the elevation of their spirits. I would see them become noble and thin . . . God, I love a Mission!

But even they could not keep me from my rendezvous with misery, for my most pressing problem was one that only I could solve. What I needed to make life worth living again was simply this: an Entrance. I have always believed that the way you first appear on stage is the way the audience will remember you for the rest of the show—perhaps, if they are the sensitive type, for the rest of their lives. Keeping this in mind, I had, on previous outings, come as a clam, as a jukebox and as a patient in a hospital bed—which was not, may I take this opportunity to say, a cheap and tasteless plea for audience sympathy, as some benighted critics have charged, but rather a bold foray into the political arena which contained within its small but swollen framework a thoughtful, even angry cry for socialized medicine.

In any case, for this new and most important of tours I needed something different; something wonderful and astonishing, yet easy to pack. Something with a message from me to all the peoples of the world. Something, above all, that would be seen as unmistakably American. I imagined myself as the Long Island Expressway; as the Grand Canyon; as a Q-Tip. But all that seemed too expected, too Holiday on Ice, if you dig my drift.

For days I feverishly racked my brain for an answer to this question of questions. Then, one afternoon, whilst I was preparing some Oscar Meyers in the kitchen, I happened to overhear the Red Sox game that Miss Frank—half deaf from endless hours of band rehearsal—had blasting on the tube. Suddenly, I realized that the answer was lying—or in this case, frying—right before my eyes.

I would come as a Hot Dog!

How brilliant! How perfect! First I'd have my girls come on as waitresses. Then I would make my grand entrance, mustard and relish glistening in the lights. I would shake my wiener, wiggle my buns. How could anyone resist such a delectable vision?

There was no stopping me. I would become the hot dog and the hot dog me. We would be as one. Like all true artists, I was determined to bring my own mighty vision before the public, no matter what that effort might entail. Let the Philistines spit on my wiener now. Time and the public would prove me right, as they had so many times before.

Of this I was blissfully, pigheadedly sure.

> "What I needed
> to make life worth living again
> was simply this: an Entrance."

DearDiary:

I just got a letter today from the Johnson Girls, two of my most loyal fans, telling me that they bought tickets for every show of mine in London and will be doing the same for all my European performances as soon as they go on sale.

I am, of course, flattered. I am also troubled.

I guess it's always troubling to be faced with that kind of devotion. Like most performers, I can deal with intense adulation from the multitudes, but as soon as it comes from a focused source . . . well, that's another matter altogether. Maybe that's why so many performer friends of mine refuse to have any dealings with even their most ardent fans. They don't want them to become specific, particularized people. Well, sometimes they hire them (they make such loyal employees), but that's just another kind of distancing as far as I'm concerned, and I've never been able to do that.

Fans. It's so tempting to dismiss their behavior as deviant or simply crazy. But when I'm actually faced with the humanity of it—the Johnson Girls, for example—there is something so essentially sweet about the whole thing, something so naive, that I find I can't dismiss it, or ignore it, or belittle it at all.

I embrace it.

Just knowing that they'll be in London or Gothenburg or wherever already makes those places less strange to me, less frightening. And what is so wonderful about the Johnson Girls in particular is that they always travel with their mother. I suppose most mothers would discourage such a consuming (and expensive!) obsession with a performer. But not theirs.

Mrs. Johnson not only encourages it, she also seems almost proud of it. For her, it is something that makes her daughters not odd, but special; not silly, but serious; not limited, but giving.

I wish you could see the three of them standing backstage after a performance, looking like they just got off the train from Boise, Idaho. Which they did. They seem to have nothing in common with the circus around them or the people around them—least of all me. Yet there they stand in all their gingham glory. So unlike anything I think I stand for. Or anyone I would ever really know. Certainly unlike anyone you'd think would ever want to know me.

But in some strange way, they give—to me—meaning. I always feel more solid, more real when they're around. They make me think that maybe there is more to me than I know.

They say they love me, the Johnson Girls do, but I love—and need—them . . . more than they'll ever know.

The Divine's Test for the Traumatized Traveler

1.

The Great Wall of China was originally built as part of:

a) a defense plan

b) a Chanukah celebration

c) a divorce settlement

d) the world's longest dog walk

2.

The Great Pyramids of Egypt are actually in:

a) Yemen

b) Lake Havasu, Arizona

c) The British Museum

d) a terrible state of disrepair

3.

The passageway leading up to the king's burial chamber in the Great Pyramid is only three feet high because:

a) that's how tall the Egyptians were

b) that's how tall the Jews were

c) The foreman was a jerk-off

d) they ran out of stepladders

e) the low ceiling forced everyone to bow as they approached the Pharaoh

4.

The Baths of Caracalla are:

a) where the nobility gathered to wash and gossip

b) a spa in Calabria known for having extremely hot water and no towels

c) the latest novel by Gore Vidal

d) a fashionable shop in Kensington specializing in brass-and-marble toilet fixtures

e) where Liza Minnelli got her start

5.

Charmant is a word the French use to describe:

a) vacationing American tourists
b) foreigners in general
c) the last ten years of the nineteenth century
d) Fats Domino
e) only themselves

6.

Upon first seeing Paris, Noël Coward was heard to exclaim:

a) Quelle ville!
b) Ou sont les garçons?
c) J'ai besoin d'un pissoir
d) Hello, sailor

7.

When in Rome, one must always:

a) do as the Romans do
b) never do as the Romans do
c) visit the Spanish Steps
d) learn the Spanish Steps
e) keep alert for a place to hide

8.

Truk is:

a) Munich's newest disco
b) A Moroccan delicacy made of cherries and lamb's wool
c) a small island in the Pacific
d) the Slavic word for "misunderstanding of a sexual nature"
e) a much-beloved Norse god responsible for herring

PART TWO

In the Following Lists, Cross Out the Word That Does Not Belong
25 Points

Bangkok, the floating market, Wat Po, Big Foot, the Emerald Buddha

Lomotil, aluminum hydroxide, miesskeit, Valium, Kaopectate

Richard the Lion-Hearted, Frederick the Great, Mad Ludwig, William the Conqueror, Crazy Eddie

Swedes, Finns, Germans, Poofters, Koreans

PART THREE

Essay Question   50 Points

n early 1978 the Indonesian island of Komodo was closed to visitors because a giant Komodo dragon went berserk and ate an American tourist. In 300 words or less deal with the following: What did the tourist look like? What was he wearing that so antagonized the reptile? Was the dragon's act a political statement? Was he acting on orders? On impulse? Is there anyone you would like to eat? See eaten? Who? Should the lizard be punished? Rewarded? What do you think this all means? Wouldn't you really rather have a Buick?

ON THE PERSONALLY DISTRESSING ASPECTS OF BEING INTERVIEWED:

——— or ———

• Character Assassination for Fun and Profit •

Oh, how I love to be interviewed! How I look forward to answering certain questions which have, since they've been asked so often, become like old friends, family even, expected company whenever the interviewer shows up, perspiring and poorly dressed, notebook open, cassette recorder recharged. Oh, those old familiar questions, questions that make me twitch with discomfort at the *déjà vu* of it all, questions that occur to members of the Fourth Estate with such killing regularity that I have often considered the possibility of a vast intrigue against me, a conspiracy to make the worst of my wit. Here I am, one of the most colorful women of my time—if not of my block—being made to sound positively legumelike in printed interviews. Now, I adore deceit and don't give a damn about being misrepresented or misquoted, but I will not be made to sound boring to the thousands who are convinced that I am, if not Jackie O, well, certainly the next-best thing. The decline in the quality of my interviews stems directly from the lack of challenging questions put to me. You'd be in the same boat if year after year you were faced with these dreary queries:

Q: How did you get your start?

What they really mean is: What was it like to work in a steam room with all those fairies dressed in towels? EEEUU! For some reason which will forever remain a mystery to me, the idea of a woman entertaining an audience dressed only in towels—an all-male audience, and homosexual, yet—is to every reporter I have ever met at once repulsive yet endlessly fascinating. They cannot hear enough of it.

This is inevitably the first question in any interview, and even though I know it's coming, I always wince when it lands. It gets very depressing, you know. I'm certain that whatever I may do in my life, whatever I may achieve, the headline of my obituary in *The New York Times* will read:

BETTE DEAD

Began Career at Continental Baths

I will now say what I pray to God will be my final word on the subject.

It was a great job and a great experience. I did *not* perform in the middle of a steam room but in the poolside cafeteria *next* to the steam room. And I always performed *en costume*. It's true that occasionally I did wear a towel. But on my head, with some bananas and cashews hanging from it, as part of my tribute to Carmen Miranda and all the fruits and nuts of the world. The audience there treated me with more respect than I deserved, considering I was brand-new at entertaining that many people, clothed or naked, for more than ten minutes at a time. My act, if you could call it that, was more like a mishmash of possibilities than the cogent, noble work I am offering nowadays. I was able to take chances on that stage I could not have taken anywhere else. Ironically, I was freed from fear by people who, at the time, were ruled by fear. And for that I will always be grateful.

And by the way, just for the record, I never laid my eyes on a single penis, even though I was looking real hard.

And this:

Q: What was it like growing up in Hawaii?

I must confess that the undying popularity of this question is entirely my fault, because I encouraged the asking of it in the first place. I thought it would amuse, and I was right. But I have lived to regret it. Lately I have begun to embroider the tale something fearful, with cockfights, Tong Wars, furious Fire Goddesses, volcanic eruptions, and escapades with all branches of the Armed Forces. This is not to say that all this embellishment is untrue, because I HARDLY EVER LIE. I do, however, forget, so here's the naked truth as well as I can recall it.

My first memories of Hawaii are of the oleander bushes that surrounded our apartment house. Their flowers gave off a sweet —almost too sweet—smell, and the white milk that spilled all over your clothes if you picked them was impossible to remove. My mother tried everything. Banana stains were rough too. But my mom wanted us to look great, and we did. We were four, three girls and one boy. My two sisters, Judy and Susan, were older than I, and my brother, Danny, is younger.

As children we were all dressed alike. My mother loved to sew, and she was terrific at it. She made all the clothes we wore, and I grew up listening to the sound of sewing machines. It was comforting to hear her go at it. In the beginning she sewed, and in the end she only mended.

The house was always littered, in the early days, with swatches of fabric and other things my mother meant to get to eventually. In one corner of the room were boxes and boxes of patterns that friends had given her, as well as cartons of rickrack, piping, laces and buttons, and a magical thread box with its rows and rows of brightly colored silk threads.

Throughout my childhood I wore the clothes she made, but I never realized what an artist she was until the day we opened the Crate. For years and years the huge wooden box stood in the living room right by the front door. My mother would never open it or tell us what was in it. Finally, when we moved to our own house and she *did* open it, she cried. It was her trousseau, and everything in it was made by hand, made by her. Beautiful quilts, embroidered with tiny stitches, sheets, dish towels, antimacassars, doilies, nighties, undies—everything. She never used any of it. It was her finest work. Her Testament to Hope.

When I turned twelve, Mom decided it was time for *me* to learn to sew. Both my sisters had had to undergo this ritual, and now it was my turn. What an ordeal! But it was worth it. Finally, I could make the clothes of my dreams, ensembles inspired by the revolutionary Mr. Frederick of Frederick's of Hollywood. It wasn't long before I was the only eighth-grader in Honolulu to come to class wearing a flawless copy of Freddie's Satin Surrender. Of course, Freddie's version was black. Mine was crimson and lilac. And how could it be otherwise?

You see, one of the most important differences between a Mainland-born American and your true Island-born wahine, such as myself, is that Mainlanders are brought up to believe that navy blue, beige and gray are the colors of good breeding and good taste, while in my part of the world those colors are worn only by clerics and dowagers. This is more significant than you may imagine, for I grew up in a blaze of color provided not only by orchids, bougainvillea, hibiscus and all sorts of other aggressively flamboyant works of nature, but by the people, who decorated themselves in ways that could blind the uninitiated eye. Yellow, aqua, orange, red, fuchsia and chartreuse was a combination I particularly favored . . . ah, *quel spectacle!*

Of course, my roots are always in evidence whenever I put a show together, because I inevitably include at least one tropical number. I took part in so many Polynesian Festivals that show biz and the hula are synonymous to me.

My first hula teacher was a lady named Kuulei Burke, and she was held in much awe because her great-great-grandmother had danced in King Kalakaua's court. She weighed in at 250 and liked to throw it around. I was not a favorite of Mrs. Burke's and was always put in the back row with the other little girls who were not so hot. I didn't care though, because I couldn't remember the steps anyway, not to mention what my hands were supposed to be doing. I always had to keep my eye on the girl next to me so I could navigate my way through the maze of movement that was Mrs. Burke's hallmark as a choreographer. If she caught anyone cheating in this fashion, she would make the poor chump stay after class and sweep up—a considerable punishment if you've ever seen the way a grass skirt sheds.

Mrs. Burke wore her hair in a large bun perched right on top of her head—very appealing if you happened to be a bird. Once when my class of utter losers was to perform at a local talent show, she insisted that we all wear our hair that way too. Mustering up the full strength of her 250 pounds, she pulled my hair up and back so tight that I had only two little slits where my eyes used to be. My usual trick for checking out the steps was completely out of the question.

As it turned out, that was the best thing that could have happened. Having absolutely no idea what the hell I was doing, I danced blindly out of the back row, knocking down several of Mrs. Burke's pets in the front, and emerged triumphant center stage. The audience roared and cheered me on. Suddenly I was in the spotlight, and I wasn't going back. I was just about to segue into a torrid little Tahitian number when two of the older girls came onstage and carried me off, kicking, into the wings.

Mrs. Burke was furious, but those few unfettered moments in the limelight were my first lesson in the power of spontaneity, and it was a lesson from which I'm still learning.

Anyway, that's what it was *really* like to grow up in Hawaii. Don't you think I should stick to the Tong Wars?

· D E A T H   B Y   R E L I S H ·

"All I needed was a great persona,
and that I could invent."

*I*t was the last day of rehearsal, and there was so much I had to do. Unfortunately, I did nothing. Instead, I spent the day stuck inside a hot dog suit.

Unbeknownst to me, the demented designers of my ten-foot marvel had used Krazy-Glu in its construction. As luck—and the lack of proper circulation inside the wiener—would have it, the glue never set properly. As soon as I stepped inside for a fitting, my just-brushed hair formed an instant and permanent bond with the rubber foam. I screamed for my hairdresser to cut me out, but he was gone, off to the *Dinah Shore Show* to discuss the carcinogenic effects of hair dyes on certain kinds of elderly rats. I couldn't just give a yank and let the hairs fall as they might. Not with my Seattle premiere only days away. There was nothing to do but wait.

It's funny, you know, the things that go through your mind while you're waiting to suffocate inside a rubber-foam wiener. Things like: "What the *hell* am I doing here?" "What was I thinking of?" And the inevitable: "I deserve this."

Needless to say, the longer I spent stuck inside that intractable hot dog, the more I became convinced that the whole thing had been a birdbrained idea to begin with. And once I questioned the hot dog, I began to question everything else I was planning to do in the show. Like my characters, for instance.

I always like to take a few characters with me when I go out on the road. They let me do things I would never be brave enough —or, some might say, stupid enough—to do under my own name. The ladies I dream up are masks I can hide behind. And I like hiding. And I like masks. In fact, I *love* masks.

Once, when I was about ten years old and as precocious as I was obnoxious, I sneaked into an out-of-the-way room in our local library that had always fascinated me. The room had no windows at all, and was dark and cool and as musty as an old dishrag. It was like no place else on the Island that I had ever seen, and I was always drawn to it, but for some reason, children were not allowed in.

On this particular day, however, the old Hawaiian guard who usually hovered menacingly by the door was not at his post. In fact, I had just seen him sitting under the big banyan tree in the courtyard staring bemusedly up at the sky. Something about the glazed look in his eyes told me he wouldn't be making an immediate return.

So in I ran. I didn't know what I wanted to do in the room exactly. Just be inside it, I suppose, because it was forbidden and because it was strange. But once in the room, my eye was caught by a book with a floridly designed cover that someone had left out on the reading table. It was called *The Decay of Lying*, and being, even then, a confirmed and joyous fibber, I wanted to see what the book had to say on the subject. I hated to think that lying, an art which I was only beginning to master, was on its way out.

Of course, the book wasn't about telling falsehoods at all. It was by Oscar Wilde and it was really about masks and how the only interesting thing about someone is the mask he wears—not the "real" person behind the mask. The *persona* was what mattered, not the person. According to Wilde, all that someone had to do to be devastatingly exciting was to make up a fabulous mask.

What a revelation! And what a relief! To have a great personality I didn't have to be a great person or even a passable one. All I needed was a great persona, and *that* I could invent. And what was most terrific of all, if someone didn't like me or what I was doing, I could always peek out from behind my mask and say, "Just kidding!" Considering how shy and basically insecure I was, Wilde certainly seemed to have the answer.

Even today, I love slipping into a new persona as much as I love slipping into a new Halston one-of-a-kind. It's much cheaper, and far more dramatic. I call my masks my "yarps," from an ancient Anglo-Saxon word meaning "woman who fishes for compliments."

Take Dolores. Or, as she is more formally known, Dolores De Lago, The Toast of Chicago, entertainer extraordinaire. I first

Dolores De Lago:
her belief in herself
is awesome.

The Magic Lady:
**optimism in the face
of everything.**

dreamed up Dolores when I saw a picture of the Little Mermaid in my Danish phrase book. What a wonderful idea for a character, I thought. A mermaid! How innocent! How vulnerable! Of course, by the time I got finished filling in the details, the innocence and vulnerability had somehow fallen by the wayside. Now I'm afraid a character sketch of Dolores would have to go something like this:

Dolores De Lago: A woman of tremendous ambition and absolutely no pride at all; a woman of tremendous determination and absolutely no skill; a woman of the grandest notions and not the simplest hint of taste. And all this wrapped up in a temperament Caligula might envy. Who else but a woman like that would dream up an act as a mermaid cavorting about the stage in an electric wheelchair, complete with swaying palms and trick coconuts? Dolores calls her act *The Revue Tropicale* and includes in it such monoliths of mediocrity as "Crackin' Up from Havin' Lack of Shackin' Up" and the inimitable "It Was Fiesta and I Had the Clap." Drawing on the lowest form of show business imaginable, the Revue's climax—if you can call it that— is the one-handed twirling of a set of Maori poi balls, a trick Dolores was taught by an itinerant sheep shearer from Wellington. She performs it with the utmost confidence. In this, as in all things, her belief in herself is awesome.

Yes, Dolores is a pretty tough cookie. But then, I have a weakness for tough cookies. In fact, the other character I thought I might drag around the world with me was a pretty rugged soul herself.

I named her "The Magic Lady," after a wheezy old bag lady who took up residence on my stoop one sodden July. At first glance, my besotted stoopmate bore about the same relationship to the human race as leftovers do to the feast the night before. But no matter how bedraggled she looked, no matter how used up she appeared—and was—she always had a feisty spark in her eye and a ready smile. Unkempt and certainly unhinged, the way she raised her bottle to me whenever I went out or came back home was somehow reassuring. Bruised and beaten, beaten and bruised, she was still doing her part to connect. When winter came and they took her away, I found I really missed her. Making up "The Magic Lady" was the way I got her back.

Unlike sassy, muttonheaded Dolores, who is, let's face it, a lot like me—or someone I might have become—The Magic Lady was, and remains, something of a stranger. Whatever parts of me she came out of are not the parts with which I'm in daily touch.

In many ways, she is the exact opposite of me, her response to experience totally different than mine: sensitive where I'd be glib; open where I'd be closed; forgiving where I'd be wailing for revenge. She sits there on that same old half-broken bench, in that same old battered coat, waving that silly umbrella, forgotten and ignored. Yet if you asked her, she'd be up in a minute, dancing around the maypole, telling you how wonderful it is to be alive and part of the human race.

And that's the part of The Magic Lady I find the most difficult to relate to: her optimism, in the face of everything. Her *enthusiasm*, which survives and survives and survives. Yet that I know is what makes her magic—and that's the part I most admire.

In any event, my masks gave me something to think about as I remained encased in my mustardy grave, my only link with life Miss Frank, who would occasionally pass Fritos and small pieces of cheese through the mouthpiece so that I might keep up my strength.

As I saw the shadows lengthen across the floor, I thought, Is this how it's going to end after all?

Headlines flashed before my eyes:

DIVA DIES IN HOT DOG MISHAP

Began Career at Continental Baths

But I have always been a lucky girl, at least when it comes to survival, and, in time, my hairdresser returned. While Miss Frank held a flashlight inside the wiener, he snipped and cut and snipped again, until, at last, I was free.

I would love to say that as I stepped out of the hot dog a giant cheer went up. But except for the girls and Miss Frank, everyone had gone.

Oh, well, I thought, that's show biz.

Dear Sis: First of all, STOP whatever you're doing and try and concentrate for five minutes. When I spoke to you last night I got the definite feeling that in typical Midler fashion your MIND WAS WANDERING. So here it is all written down just in case you forget.

No. 1: The turntable I ordered for Daniel should be arriving in New York in a few days. Please pick it up and send it to him right away. It's his going-away present. Mom and Pop's present I'm sending from here—my maid, Aretha. Aretha and Mama should get along famously—they both hate to clean.

I never understood why it's the people who go away who get the goodies. It's the ones left behind that need cheering up. So I decided to give everyone going-away presents. Write a nice little note to Daniel, will ya? Tell him I miss him and love him and try to explain what I'm doing—as if I knew.

No. 2: Go to Bloomingdale's—third floor. Walk past all the Ultrasuede. Continue on through Junior Miss past all the beauty-hint books by Continental ladies of dubious titles, no matter what vegetable they are suggesting you smear on your face. Just past the book stand you will see a small barred window marked GIFT WRAPPING. Sitting behind the bars there will be a remarkably ill-tempered young man remarkably misnamed Mr. Merth, who will, if you state your name clearly and in no way disturb his day, present you with a large box containing your going-away present. And you'd better like it, bitch. Right now I need all the encouragement I can get.

I wish you could leave your class in the hands of a sub for a few days and come to London. I asked Mom and Pop, but I think the trip was just too much for them. You know my manager wants me to end the tour in Hawaii. He thinks it would make great copy to end where I began, etc. etc. But I don't really want to do it. I mean if a prophet is without honor in his own country, what about a loudmouth like me? I'm always afraid Mrs. Burke will suddenly appear, and picking me up by the back of the neck like some great tabby, announce to one and all, "This hussy is a fraud!"

In any event, I must be off and slogging once again through the Paleozoic slime that will be my life until we get this turkey on its feet. I sent you a copy of my itinerary, so you have no excuse not to write. I'll even write back. If I don't come running back first.

Try and come to London for the opening. But if you can't, I understand. Just remember to say a little prayer for me about 11 A.M. your time on the morning of the 18th of September. Younger sisters still get scared.

All my love as always,

Bette

Reprinted from the
SEATTLE BULLETIN-HERALD

Mad, Bad and Dangerous to Know:

An Interview with The Divine Miss M

REPORTER: Good afternoon, Miss M. Welcome to Seattle.

MISS M: Oh, is it afternoon? Already?

REPORTER: Almost night, actually.

MISS M: Imagine that.

REPORTER: I wonder, could you tell us, how did you get your start? (MISS M leaves. She has her maid ask me to leave. I am dumbstruck. I weep, plead. I cajole. I offer to take her to eat Chinese. MISS M returns.) Well, perhaps we should move on. Do you expect to have any problems with language as you go from country to country?

MISS M: *Au contraire.* I'm looking forward to it. I love a little foreign tongue now and then, don't you?

REPORTER: Oh . . . uh . . . certainly. Certainly. Actually, it has been rumored that you have learned 3 or 4 words in six or seven languages in 8 or 9 weeks. If this is true, it would be a stunning feat.

MISS M: Not at all! For me, thorough preparation is a way of life. *Semper pour la monde,* as the French like to say. One does what one must do. I have never been a believer in the easy way out.

REPORTER: I—

MISS M: Except perhaps in the case of fire, in which instance a quick and facile exit is not just appropriate; it's advisable.

REPORTER: Well, besides your language studies, what else are you doing to prepare for what must be, even by your standards, a most ambitious undertaking?

MISS M: I'm taking a lot of vitamins, reading Gibbons' later works on feudal vestiges in postindustrial Europe and trying desperately to get my hands on some speed. You wouldn't by any chance . . . ?

REPORTER: Uh . . . I'm afraid not. But tell me, is there any country you are particularly excited about visiting?

MISS M: Oh, yes. Japan.

REPORTER: Japan? But Japan isn't on your itinerary.

MISS M: It isn't? Oh, well. (MISS M shouts raucously to some unseen person.) Miss Frank! Scrap the Jap drag! We ain't going!

REPORTER: Is there any other country you are particularly interested in?

MISS M: I'm interested in them all. Individually and as a cohesive unit. The Old World versus the New, don't you see? I want to compare and contrast. I want to understand what I am by seeing what others are . . . (The Divine takes a sip of Perrier.)

REPORTER: How interesting.

MISS M: . . . wearing.

REPORTER: Oh.

MISS M: It's so hard to get it all from *Vogue*, you know. You have to be there. Try things on.

REPORTER: Oh, I thought you meant something else. May I ask how rehearsals are going?

MISS M: There *are* no problems and there will *be* no problems.

REPORTER: Is that true?

MISS M: I never know how much of what I say is true. If I did, I'd bore myself to death.

REPORTER: Well, if anyone can bring it off, you can. Do you work hard at being the best in your field?

MISS M: People are not the best because they work hard. They work hard because they are the best.

REPORTER: Oh?

MISS M: It's a matter of responsibility. To your talent, my dear. Of course, I don't consider myself the best in any-

thing. Except perhaps the trying on and proper selection of footwear. A pretty foot, you know, is a gift of nature. Goethe said that.

REPORTER: Goethe? You're familiar with the works of Goethe?

MISS M: Only the parts about feet.

REPORTER: I see. Well, just a few more questions.

MISS M: Ask on, Macduff. And damn'd be him that first cries, "Hold, enough!"

REPORTER: Well, my question is: What, in the long run, do you expect to get out of this tour?

MISS M: I don't know WHAT to expect. That's why I'm doing it.

REPORTER: Well, then, just one more question: Are you confident that what you do—onstage, I mean—will be understood and appreciated by non-Americans?

MISS M: I'm as confident as Cleopatra's pussy.*

E · D · I · T · O · R · S · N · O · T · E

* Miss M has a way of throwing this allusion into interviews whenever questioned or challenged on some point of inner security. It has already been established beyond any reasonable doubt that Cleopatra never had a pussy; or if she did, no one ever saw it; or if anyone did see it, they were not impressed enough to remark on it in writing. It must, therefore, be assumed that Miss M's use of this expression is nothing more than a smoke screen to hide her real feelings; a red herring of a soul, if you will. Or if you won't, just another example of this woman's total disregard for the simplest rules of civilized conversation.

In any case, I can only beg you not to cancel your subscription to this paper, which pledges, here and now, that we will *never* print another word about this absurd woman of whom one can only say what Lady Caroline said of Byron so many years ago: "Mad, bad and dangerous to know.")

I n Seattle, that hilly, chilly city of the North which spreads out like lumpy pancake batter along the placid shores of the octopus-ridden Puget Sound, we had our first out-of-town tryout. At least, *I* was certainly trying to get out of town. I couldn't believe that we had to be ready for the public in just two days. Everything and everyone was in disarray or disrepute. My staff and crew, upon whom I so heavily rely in times of crisis, were relying heavily on me. And all I wanted to do was drive up

to Vancouver. Ah, Vancouver! I played there once, and while I was singing "Superstar," a ballad of ineffable longing and several modulations, someone hit me in the mouth with a bagel. I like to go back there every now and then to remember where things are *really* at.

But being one who never flees from a battle unless she has a confirmed first-class ticket, I remained at the helm. And what a ship I had to steer! And through what murky waters!

And all because of a new and devastating dilemma: Except for the Hot Dog, I had nothing to wear. I was either too thin or too

> "If I don't feel right about what I'm in, I don't feel right about anything."

fat for my old clothes, and the new clothes I'd had made were unthinkable, ranging from a Tribute—to—Bacchus number in hot-pink polyester peckered all over with vine leaves and plastic grape clusters, to an ensemble my designer called Man's Best Friend, made from a Dalmatian-print polyester and complete with rhinestone collar and leash. How could I have let myself be talked into any of it?

I was desperate. Clothes were, and are, as important to me as an Entrance. If I don't feel right about what I'm in, I don't feel right about anything. Every minute, every hour I should have spent rehearsing I spent getting into and out of clothes. I was needed onstage for a lighting check, for a sound check, for a music rehearsal, for a run-through. And still I was up in my dressing room, trying on this with that; wrapping a belt here; sticking a flower there; putting things on backwards, upside down, inside out. And of course, each new invention had to be tried on with twenty different pairs of shoes. Maybe a spiked heel would make it work. Maybe a low one. Boots? Sneakers? Shower shoes? Nothing helped.

My wardrobe dilemma brought everything to a standstill. And the time pressure was enormous. Tempers flared. Fights broke out. Some threatened to quit if I didn't come out of the dressing room. Finally, having no other choice, I swallowed my pride and called my designer in Los Angeles, the nut who'd made the clothes I loathed so much, and begged him to come to Seattle. Always the soul of honesty, I told him he'd be walking into an atmosphere charged with tension.

"Nothing fazes me" was all he said.

When he arrived, that very same evening, he looked like the brash young man in his late twenties that he was. But a mere twenty-four hours later, he was unrecognizable. His entire body sagged. The flesh fell from his eyes. His face became wrinkled and puffy. If you asked him for the time or the salt, he would cry. His gait, once so confident and strong, became halting. His hands began to shake. At the end of rehearsal, we carried him sobbing to his hotel room, where he spent the night sewing— the sheets to the bedspread; the towels to the shower curtain; his shoes to his socks.

Oh, it was not an easy time. For any of us. Only Miss Frank, exhausted though she was from zipping and unzipping, hemming and unhemming, was able to smile. In fact, she seemed very pleased with herself, forever mumbling in my ear about just deserts and the terrible wages of sin.

But as is so often the case in a business where you lose fifty grand if it doesn't, the show *did* go on. Two hours late and in a shambles, but a show nevertheless. The audience was, as most audiences usually are, unthinkably patient and forgiving. Dolores and The Magic Lady were ragged but wonderful. The crowd even liked my dog dress, which I actually wore and which became the surprise hit of the evening, retrieving for my designer both his reputation and his youth.

Of course, I kept telling myself, trying not to let the elation go to my head, this was still America, home sweet home. The real test lay about six thousand miles away. In London. And that night of reckoning was getting closer by the second.

> "*. . . in a business where you lose fifty grand if it doesn't, the show did go on.*"

PALLADIUM LONDON STOP AM ON MY WAY STOP ARRIVING MOMENTARILY STOP TALLY HO STOP BETTE

· O P E N I N G   N I G H T ·

"I'm just crazy about royalty,
especially queens."

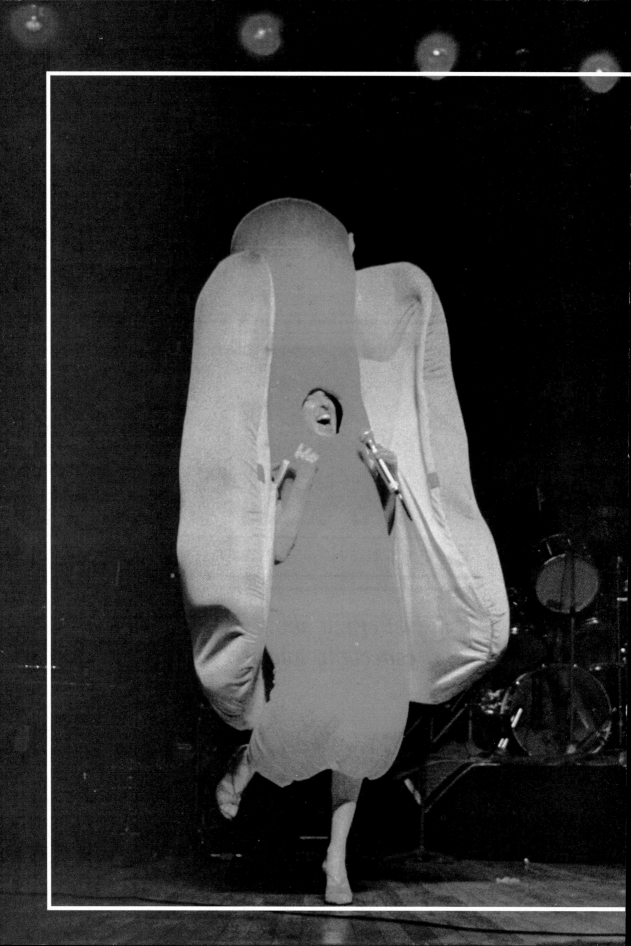

THE LONDON PALLADIUM

THE LONDON PALLADIUM

*O*h, my, my! London! At last! What a thrill it is to be here playing the Palladium right in the very heart of The Old UK— or The YUK, as we sometimes call it. Well, there'll always be an England, they say. Tonight we put that to the ultimate test. Oh, I tell you, we are so excited. We have done it all. We read our Shakespeare. We boned up on Blake. We read Milton till we went blind. I did so want to impress you all. Unfortunately, I don't speak Arabic. Well, at least I haven't had any trouble with the metric system. We've gone metric too, you know. It was a difficult transition to make. So many of us had been thinking in inches for so many, many years. And you know, while we're in London we're hoping to meet the Royal Family. I don't know why it is, but every time I hit a town the blue-bloods all seem to flee to their summer residences. I can't imagine why. I'm just crazy about royalty, especially queens. Your Queen, for example, Elizabeth the Second . . . Elizabeth the Tooth, we call her. My dears, she is the whitest woman of them all. She makes us all feel like the Third World. I only have one question to ask Her Maj:

"What have you got in that handbag?" . . . *Oh, I tell you, I love her. I'd kill to get my hands on one of her hats. Such unerring taste. Who do you think makes those hats for her, anyway? She's probably got a little hat fairy chained to the basement saying, "Queenie's gonna love this one!" His specialty is special hats for special occasions. I was lucky enough to see one of them. It's called The Last Supper. It has twelve little apostles about the brim and little pieces of matzoh hanging down about the ears. It's her Easter number. . . . And of course, I just adore Charles. Do you think I stand a chance in this hot dog suit? I read somewhere that he can marry a commoner. I guess he wouldn't want someone as common as my own self. . . . Well, some of us are losers and some of us are wieners. But you know, my very favorite of all is Princess Anne. Such an active lass. So outdoorsy. She loves nature in spite of what it did to her. Oh, my God! Did I say that? I didn't say that. Dare I go on? . . . All right. How many of you would like to see my impression of Princess Anne? . . . Hmmm. Now, if I can only get out of this sausage drag. . . .*

*E*ver since I first saw Greer Garson show Laurence Olivier how to shoot an arrow in *Pride and Prejudice*, I have been an avid Anglophile. So you can imagine how I looked forward to seeing all those famous English landmarks that had excited my imagination for so long: the Tower, with its cache of royal jewels I not only adored but coveted; the brooding moors where Emily Brontë walked in gloom and sensible shoes; the Albert Memorial with its stirring salute to Engineering; and, of course, Stonehenge. To my amazement, I soon discovered that they were all hundreds of miles apart from each other. I guess before one actually visits them, everyone tends to think of their favorite countries as one grand Disneyland filled with national monuments and historical treasures conveniently laid out for easy viewing, when what they really are filled with, of course, is people going to work, laundromats and places to buy rat poison. The realization that England was not just an efficiently organized museum was at first disappointing, then exhilarating, then disappointing again as I counted how few days I had to see it all. Faced with such a plethora of things to see and do, I had to decide where to go first. And I had to decide fast. Charles Jourdan seemed like a good idea.

Donning a gray knit cap that hung somewhat awkwardly down one side of my jaw, a pair of sunglasses that hid my eyes and a long woolen scarf which completely covered the lower half of my face, I stepped sweating into the English sunshine, blind as a bat and unable to breathe, but completely unrecognizable.

I felt these precautions necessary because of the tremendous success I had been in that tasteful town of swans and swains. In fact, when I wasn't busy doing TV shows or radio spots, I was aflitter with parties and celebrations given in honor of my recent ascension to the English Theatrical Throne, an ascension which had taken everyone by surprise, especially me. Inevitably, of course, the good wishes and good feelings expressed by those present at Parties and Celebrations thrown to honor somebody else's success are as forced as the mincemeat one is often made to eat at them. But being as great a lover of fakery and fraud as I am of accusation and scandal, I had a grand old time.

So my decision to go to Charles Jourdan was not completely frivolous. I needed a new pair of shoes for yet another *fête* to which I had been invited by a very noble group of English men and women who thought I might be amusing for an afternoon.

Oh, yes, what a *rara avis* I was to those who had never been to the slums of Honolulu. I provided them with such delight. You should have heard this particular bunch gasp and swoon when I stuck two fingers into my bowl of haggis, mistaking it for a bowl of poi, a gloplike staple of the Islands. How I regaled them with tales of the South Pacific and the North Bronx. And how they regaled me with their stories of Forthright Industrial Action and the Truth about Ale.

After luncheon, things really picked up. I was quietly staring at an enormous painting of the lady of the house, trying to decide if she was holding in her lap a small dog or a rat with a bow in its hair, when a young woman of serious demeanor approached me. I'd say she was about thirty-five and had never been—or, having been, was disappointed. She was all in black wool except for a red hat topped all over with what appeared to be a *salade niçoise*. As she approached, I could see a solid determination in her eyes that seemed totally at odds with the whimsical hat. In fact, everything about her was about as solid as solid can get. As she came striding towards me, she held out her hand for me to shake. Fearful of what she might do to my fingers, I gingerly gave her only two.

"I'm Cecily," she said as she relaxed her grip.

"Bette Midler," I responded in my most English Garden manner.

"I know," Cecily said, "of course. That's why I'm *so* anxious to speak with you."

She practically towed me into a quiet corner.

"Well, darling," she said to me in that tone the English consider chatty, "I have the most *extraordinary* idea. I want to use *your* face and *your* money in what I consider a daring—and brilliant—scheme of mine to produce a special designer line of diaphragms and douches."

I looked around to see if anyone had heard. Then I had to laugh. But Cecily was dead serious, and her reason for thinking the venture worthwhile was a most curious blend of politics, hedonism and outright greed.

"The diaphragm," she told me over high tea, "is an object that heralds pleasure. Why must it look like some hideous prosthetic device that just came out of a hospital supply room? Ditto, you see, for the douche. Is there any reason," she went on firmly, her tomatoes bouncing up and down in place, "that these items, so intimately connected with feminine delight, should be not only unattractive, but positively *repellent*? Think about it, darling. Isn't this state of affairs the result of a sexist, puritanical society still resisting the idea that sex for a woman can be a beautiful, joyous occasion free of guilt and anxiety?"

I must say I was intrigued. Old Lettuce Head was really hip. Sensing my interest, Cecily nibbled on a scone and went on.

"There is no doubt in my mind, dear. What the world needs

> "... *what a* rara avis *I was to those who had never been to the slums of Honolulu.*"

56

now is a hand-painted diaphragm and douche set that comes complete with its own design-coordinated carrying case—you know, something a woman would be proud to take anywhere. Of course, what's most important . . . Are you following, dear? What are you staring at?"

"Your veggies, Cecily. They seem to be heading for a tumble."

"Oh, bother," Cecily said, readjusting her hat, which by now had slipped down nearly to her nose, "what a *nuisance* vanity can be. But I was saying, in actual point of fact, what's most important is that when she reaches inside that colorful little case, a woman will not be met by the sight of an ugly medicinal-looking device designed as if pleasure were a sin, but instead by a lovely, artful item designed specifically *for* pleasure. . . . Well, speak up. What do you think?"

But before I had a chance to let her know, Cecily raved on.

"I've already decided on several themes I thought might translate jolly well as design lines for the sets. I'm thinking particularly of a line I call Miss Liberty. I will have the bust of the famous bronze statue painted boldly on the diaphragm, while the refillable douche dispenser will be in the very shape of the great lady herself. On the case I would have a full-length portrait of the Torchbearer. Think, darling, what that would *mean* to a woman. After that, I'm considering a series based on other feminine interests such as Louis the IV Furniture, Lovers on the Run and of course, Famous Women of the Twentieth Century. And here, my dear, is where you come in. You see, I think your portrait would look simply smashing on a diaphragm. Your hair would so nicely fill out the circular design of the device itself. Don't you agree? . . .

"Of course," Cecily continued, hardly giving me a chance to comprehend what I'd just heard, "there'll be no more calling things diaphragms and douches. I'm going to call my items DIDOs, after the famous queen."

Somewhere in the back of my mind I seemed to recall that Dido killed herself unloved and untouched, but I thought it best not to mention that to Cecily.

"You see," the indomitable woman went on, "names are everything. Not just for people. For things too. Take death, for example."

"Death?" I queried, failing to see the immediate connection between death and feminine hygiene.

"Yes. People are afraid of death, so they call it by every other name they can think of. They talk about pushing up the daisies, or checking out, or croaking, or popping off, or hopping the

57

twig, or cashing in one's chips, or joining the Choir Invisible. Death by any other name *is* sweeter. Juliet, darling, beautiful though she may have been, failed to grasp an essential truth."

Oh, Cecily, I thought as a slowdown in the hat bobbing indicated she was finally coming to a halt, what a scamp you are! Then when I was certain she was through, I told her I'd consider everything she said and fled out the door, my mind reeling.

My but it had been an edifying afternoon! How I regretted that my three yentas had not been there with me to listen and learn. They were in their hotel rooms, with shades drawn, recovering. London, you see, had proved to be a bit rough for them.

As you may remember, I had promised to see to my girls' cultural refinement, and towards that goal had surprised them with tickets to a special National Theatre matinee of *Hedda Gabler*. But the tickets went unused. Worse than unused. Sold. For a dank afternoon in an East Thamesian bar where the hapless girls were arrested for attempting to raffle off some personal items they had snatched off my dressing table. Unfortunately, a few of those items were illegal in Great Britain, so the girls got more than they bargained for. A trial date, for example.

The remainder of my troupe were adjusting to life on foreign soil with varying degrees of success. My band, as usual, didn't know *where* they were, so there was nothing for them to adjust to. With the notable exception of my drummer, Doane, who nearly blew himself up one night trying to get the water heater to work, they remained as unruffled and inscrutable as ever.

And then there was Miss Frank. Considering my dresser's puritanical aversion to Pomp and Grandeur, I had feared that upon our arrival in London, she might very well take to her room and limit her communication with me to reproachful notes full of apocalyptic foreboding and advice. But such was not to be. Perhaps it was the aroma of rotting cod wafting up from the Fish and Chips shop below, or the fact that such a large part of the populace was considerate enough to speak in English. Whatever the reasons, if London contained any failures of the human spirit, Miss Frank forgave them all and flourished like a rose in Paddington.

How I hated to leave the town where things—on the whole—had gone so well for me. But as it often does just when I'm enjoying myself, Duty called, and before I even had a chance to say But-isn't-Brighton-in-Brooklyn? I was packed again and wending my way south toward the rocky shores of the English Channel.

*W*ell, the fog's lifting

The sand's shifting

I'm drifting on out

Old Captain Ahab's longing to hear from me,

Swallow me,

Don't follow me,

I'm traveling alone

Blue water's my daughter

I skip like a stone, . . .

*A*nd now,
Ladies and Germs,
would you
please give a
rousing welcome
to three prime
examples of why
drugs are not
the answer.
Just back from
the Brighton Pier,
where they
are one of the rides,
please say hello
to the Staggering
Harlettes!!!!!

"It's the best..."
—Sir Walter Raleigh

QUEEN ARMS HOTEL

LONDON SW 14 ENGLAND

Dear Peter:

Darling, don't worry about the car. At least you didn't kill anyone! You know how they drive. If you live in Beverly Hills they don't put blinkers in your car. They figure if you're that rich you don't have to tell people where you're going. It's not driving anymore, honey, it's primal therapy. In the three years we've been together in that land of billboards and burritos I haven't honked my horn once—I just stick my head out the window and scream.

I received your letters in Lund. I'm <u>still</u> not sure where it is. Do you think in years to come when people in show business want to know the mettle of their material they'll ask, "Yes, but will it play in Lund?" Lund, my god. "Friends, Romans, and Countrymen—Lund me your ears."

There! You see what's happening to me? With Virtue guarding my mind, and Miss Frank guarding my door, I miss you more than ever.

Your everlovin'
sometimes blondie

Bette

· CHOPPED HERRING ·

"I eat, therefore I am . . ."

DIVINE REVELATIONS, Chapter 1 : Verse 1

Nana was just about to receive the "Golden Fly" award when Flight 54 nose-dived through the clouds and suddenly there was Sweden. My first impression was that the pilot had defected to the East and we were about to land in Siberia. Every city girl's vision of ultimate wilderness lay spread out below me: nothing but row upon row of the darkest, most perfectly triangular pines marching relentlessly off to the horizon, their green undulations broken here and there by small black lakes and racing rivers. Not a road, not a farm, not even a Howard Johnson's to indicate that man had ever been there or ever planned to be. It was beautiful but disturbing, for as we headed down for a landing I couldn't help wondering where the six thousand people I was supposed to play for that night were going to come from. Still, this *was* my Arrival on the Continent, and I refused to allow the fact that we seemed to be landing in some remote time-forgotten wilderness to dampen my excitement. Instead, I let my soul swell with the pioneer spirit, and trying desperately to remember if I knew any jokes about lumber or canoeing, I lifted up my satchel and my chin and disembarked.

The airport was a shock. As modern and civilized as any I'd ever seen: poured concrete and recessed lighting, the latest in contemporary graphics, an architectural non sequitur delightful in its total inappropriateness to its surroundings. Actually, the airport did have one thing in common with its environment: there was not a human being in sight. Maybe the promoter had said I was going to play for six thousand raccoons; maybe this was all a gigantic mistake, due, no doubt, to some faulty trans-atlantic cable or the lilting peculiarities of the Swedish accent. Discouraged, but still determined, I kicked a possum off my luggage and walked through towering blue spruces to the bus that was waiting to take us to the theatre, smiling bravely on my way at my troupe, all of whom seemed as astonished as I to have landed in Siberia.

But eventually, as we drove toward the town that had to be there somewhere, the pines began to give way to farms, then to small clumps of houses, until from the knoll of a hill I could see something totally unexpected: the North Sea. And there, stretched out along its edge, like a rampart between the forest and the ocean, was a city.

Well, not exactly a city. But it was too late to be choosy.

Jutebory, or Gothenburg, or Göteborg—everyone pronounced

> *"Jutebory . . .*
> *was the Swedish equivalent*
> *of Des Moines."*

it differently and every sign spelled it differently—was the Swedish equivalent, it turned out, of Des Moines. My manager had decided to kick off the Continental portion of my tour here so that if we bombed miserably at least we could hide our heads in a compost heap and maybe fix up the act before we got to the big burgs.

But even as we started to drive into what was, thank God, quite a large town, I found it hard to believe that anyone in Jutebory would lay down good money to see some demented American in a dog dress do a two-bit impression of Shelley Winters. I felt yet another loss of heart coming on when suddenly we turned onto the main drag of town and, amazingly enough, into a sea of teen-agers who, like so many of their rural or small-town counterparts in America, seemed to have nothing to do with the staid, conservative territory around them.

Yet there they were—greased-back hair, tight tight jeans, black leather jackets—and the motorcycles to go with them. When we arrived on Friday evening, bikeloads of Sha-na-na look-alikes were cruising up and down, shouting what I took to be obscenities and/or traffic reports at the girls, who were also in motorcycle jackets and evidently loving every minute of the abuse. Well, maybe my Jutebory engagement wouldn't be a disaster after all.

My breast swelled with hope and curiosity. As soon as the bus pulled up to the hotel I hopped right out, and before anyone could stop me, I went for a walk on my own.

I didn't get very far. Right across the street was a brightly colored food stall, with the legend M. Svenson emblazoned on a big yellow-and-blue umbrella. Famished after the pathetic little *pâté en croûte* Air France considered *déjeuner*, I looked both ways in the wrong direction and dashed through the traffic, my mouth watering.

"Hello," I said cheerily to the neat little man behind the counter.

"*Goddag. Det skall bli ett nöje,*" he replied, tipping his hat and making a little bow, "*att hjälpa er.*"

"Oh," I replied charmed by the vendor's Continental politeness. "Do you speak English?"

"*Nej, nej. Vad önskar ni?*"

Well, at least I could tell he had asked a question. Remembering Miss Frank's adage that a pointing finger is worth a month at Berlitz, I smiled and pointed to a tray of chopped herring that looked irresistible.

"*Nej! Nej!*" Mr. Svenson cried. "*Ni måste välja!*"

And then *he* began to point. Up in the air. I couldn't figure out what he was pointing at. Then I saw it: above the stall was a large sign picturing all the various herring combinations available. There were little drawings of plain herring, herring with onions, herring with cucumbers, herring with carrots; of chopped herring, of chopped herring with apples, chopped herring with mustard, chopped herring with garlic and mustard. Faced with those forty-odd pictures, that waving finger and my innate fear of vendors, all I could do was quiver dumbly in my new caribou boots and stand there, dazed with the possibilities of herring.

"*Ni måste välja!*" Mr. Svenson repeated, snapping me out of my reverie.

Throwing caution to the wind, I decided on No. 36—chopped herring with onions and cucumbers on some kind of bread—and pointed firmly at the appropriate drawing.

Unfortunately, as his rolling eyes told me, Mr. Svenson couldn't *see* the sign. It was too high and too far back. Oh, well,

*"Remembering
Miss Frank's adage that
a pointing finger is worth
a month at Berlitz . . ."*

I thought, I'll simply point at each tray, and with my stomach grumbling wildly, I began to do so.

Mr. Svenson became more hopped up than ever. *"Ni måste bli precis!"* he exclaimed practically in tears, as he feverishly pointed upward once again.

"But why? *Why* can't I point at the *trays?*" I whined almost in tears.

"Amerikanare är förryckt!" was all the vendor muttered, as he threw down his spoon in a frigid display of Nordic disgust.

"You know," I said in that calm tone which sounds like a truce but is really a declaration of war, "here I am, newly arrived in your country, anxious only to think the best of your fair land, eager to praise the Swedish mind, the Swedish heart. But I am not only open-minded. I am also starving. So I come to you in friendship and I ask you, as one human being to another, WHY CAN'T I POINT AT THE TRAYS, YOU MISERABLE LITTLE . . ."

At this strategic point, I felt a hand on my shoulder. I turned around to look into the eyes of Max von Sydow. At least, I thought it was Max. He sure looked stern enough.

"Young lady," the stranger said, "you wish to know why you cannot just point at the trays?"

"Well," I mumbled incoherently, eyeballing his *sensational* fur coat, "yes."

"Then I tell you. You see, you didn't come to just any fish stall. You have come to the most famous fish stall in all of Jutebory. In all of Sweden perhaps. Mr. Svenson here is a man of pride, of genius. He would never serve you anything that was not perfect. And of course in food, as in life, order is everything."

It is? I thought, remembering some of the chow I had thrown together in the past.

"Now, what combination did you want?" the stranger asked me.

"Number 36."

"All right, then, you were pointing at the cucumbers, were you not?"

I had to admit that I was.

"Well, if Mr. Svenson had put the cucumbers on the bread *before* the onions, the result would have been a soggy mess. Unthinkable. You see, to prepare a dish properly, the chef must know what *all* the ingredients are going to be. Mr. Svenson was only acting out of a sense of duty. To his reputation and the continuing education of your palate. And now, if you will allow me . . ."

My well-dressed friend spoke to Mr. Svenson, who rapidly began putting together a platter.

"Here," the stranger said when Mr. Svenson was done. "Number 36. Chopped herring with cucumbers and onions."

"Why, thank you," I said quite touched. "May I pay you for—"

"Of course not," the man said. "I hope you enjoy Scandinavia. I know you'll enjoy the fish."

And with that he was off. Savoring the concoction, I looked back at Mr. Svenson, who was already tipping his hat to another customer.

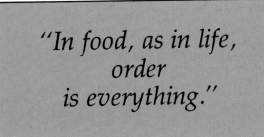

"In food, as in life, order is everything."

The Most Famous Fish Stall in all of Jutebory. Well, go know. I finished my herring rapt in thought and resolved thenceforth to bear in mind while traveling that it is best to always assume, until proved otherwise, that the fish stall you are in is the most famous of them all, and the man you are speaking to, a hero.

*I*had always wanted to see the Scandanavian countries. But not from the middle of an ice rink. Yet that's what I was playing in Jutebory, and there I was, teeth chattering, in the locker room of the hometown hockey team. Miss Frank, whose fingers were too numb to sew, had given up the needle and resorted to glue. She sat huddled in a corner, trying to paste some renegade sequins onto Dolores' tail, while I sat staring into my dressing-room mirror, not only shivering, but terrified at what I was about to face: my first non–English-speaking audience. I could see it all before me—hordes of thundering reindeer-chomping Swedes rising up as one and walking out, impatient with and/or repelled by what they could not understand. The vision was enough to drive even the strongest of divas to drink or worse. Unfortunately, since we had to cross a different border every day, I had neither drink nor worse at hand.

What was I to do? Running away seemed like a pretty good idea, but I was in my bathrobe and loath to ask Miss Frank for anything in her present state. Lately, she had been even stranger than usual. I think 86-ing the hot dog really got to her. What with all those hours of relish sewing and mustard patching, I suspect the poor woman had developed an intense attachment to the wiener and was, consequently, bummed out when the old skinless bit the dust. And after all, her name was Frank, so that might have had something to do with it too.

I have learned to discard no possibilities in my efforts to discover what's really going on.

But let's face it: the hot dog had to go. In fact, I was still recovering from that indelible moment during my third performance in London when I stepped out to sing "Lullaby of Broadway" and, without warning, my buns fell off. Right on top of the Duke of B. . . . How could I ever chance that sausage suit again? We left its remains in London, crumpled up and unrecognizable in an alley near the theater, to the deep disappointment of some and the great relief of others.

I, of course, had my own special reaction to the frankfurter's demise. In what I'm sure was some sort of psychological counterattack, I felt compelled to eat every wurst I saw. And in Sweden, you see a lot of wursts. In fact, they have as many different kinds of wursts as they do herring: fat wursts, skinny wursts, wursts with sauerkraut and wursts with potatoes, wursts with cucumbers and wursts with herring. Cold wursts and hot wursts, long wursts and short wursts, the best wursts and the worst wursts, I consumed them all.

So it is not surprising that as I sat there in Jutebory, in that room redolent with jockism, terrified, freezing, and gnawing on the last wurst in town, I desperately needed something to lighten my spirits. But I could think of only one thing that might help: A victim. Someone, anyone, on whom I could vent my misery. But who?

My musical director seemed an excellent target. His skin was as thick as a rhino's. I was certain he could stand a bombardment

> . . the best wursts and the worst wursts, I consumed them all."

that would send any normal human being fleeing for his life.

Unfortunately, as soon as I called him in, I saw that his right arm was in a sling and his left eye was covered with a large square of gauze which he had attached to his forehead with a length of black electrical tape. Clearly, he and his *petite amie* had had another row. Even for me, he was too lame a target to make any further injury enjoyable. "Do you want to go over some tunes?" he asked through a pair of extraordinarily swollen lips.

"I want to kill," I responded.

He understood. "But I am already dead," he said. And then, laying my music down before me, out he ran, bellyaching, into the frigid hallway.

And still I had no outlet for my pent-up emotions. I tried singing my scales, brushing my hair, even running through stage one of my semi—classical semi—dance movements. Nothing helped. I *had* to have a victim. Just then my manager walked smiling into the room.

One look into my eyes and he knew that his best move was a quick exit. But I had him. "Why an ice rink?" I screamed. "Why this town I never heard of? Why must my dresser and I be made

"I'm going to go out there and turn that ice rink into a wading pool!"

to freeze like match girls in the snow?'' I hurled each question at him like a knife, but he didn't even flinch.

Clearly, words were not enough. Crazed with the need to do damage, I reached behind me for something to throw at that face of tempered steel.

When I came to, about fifteen minutes later, they told me I was lucky to be alive. I had somehow managed, in reaching behind me for a weapon, to stick my finger directly into the electrical converter that was lying on my table, waiting to receive my hair dryer. At first, as I lay sprawled out over the rouge and depilatories, everyone thought I was dead. Now they were concerned that I felt no ill effects.

Ill effects? One look in the mirror and I felt terrific. The shock

had lent a certain becoming color to my cheeks, curled my hair, and left me with a warm, tingling sensation where before there had been only chills and shivering. Furthermore, except for Miss Frank, who stood off to one side mumbling how this was only the beginning, everyone was standing around me, being so solicitous and attentive that every self-absorbed, self-centered fiber of my being was appeased and purring happily.

Now I could go out and face those thundering, non–English-speaking Swedes. Let them walk out on me! Let them not understand! I had my friends! My family! I needed nothing more!

"Come, Miss Frank," I bravely cried, flinging my split ends over my shoulder, "cinch me in! And make it tight! I'm going to go out there and turn that ice rink into a wading pool! . . . If I only knew a little more Swedish . . ."

Good Evening Ladies and Germs and welcome to another breathless evening of Tit and Wit! I stand before you nipples to the wind, ready to please you in every way you hoped I might and some you hoped I might not. . . . Am I talking too fast? Am I talking too slow? . . . In honor of my first trip to the North Countries, I come to you tonight mean as Scrooge and twice as horny, full of stories, songs and little pieces of exotic information you might not have known had you not bought a ticket to see this demented demiblonde. Ain't that right, girls? How many of you think I'm still talking too fast? . . . How many vote for too slow? . . . How many of you think I should just shut up and go home? . . . Where was I? Oh, the girls. Look at those girls. The new lot. Each and every one of them a former Miss Matjes Herring. New girls, but the same old drag. You know me, honey, I am the Queen of Recycling! We didn't have auditions to find these three—we had fittings . . . but I tell you, I am as proud as a peahen over these three yentas. Notice I did not say peacock. My consciousness has been raised. But I suggest you take notice of it right away, as there will be less and less evidence of it as the evening wears on. . . . Am I talking all right now? . . . Is everything okay? . . .

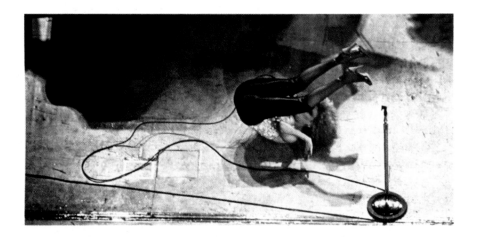

After our tremendous success in Jutebory I sensed a subtle change in my girls. Their worldly success had gone completely to their heads, and I thought that a walk through the tawdry carnival nightlife of Liseberry, the local amusement park, might remind them of what they once had been, and might easily become again—if they displeased the Gods (or Goddesses).

PART I

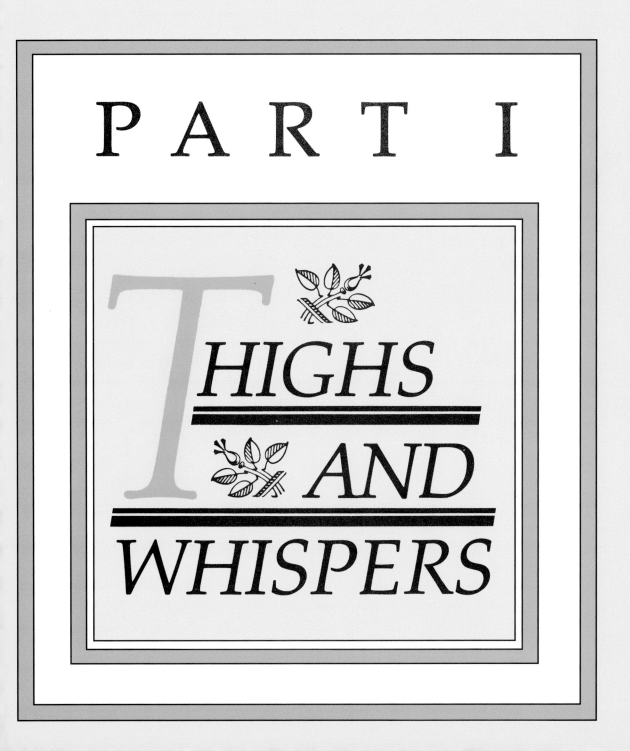

THIGHS AND WHISPERS

*I*t all began reasonably enough. As there were only two flights out of Gothenburg to Stockholm, one at 8 A.M. (too early) and one at 6 P.M. (too late), a private plane was hired to take The Divine and Miss Frank to the distant Swedish capital. The plane, a Cessna six-seater, was scheduled to leave at noon, and at noon (thanks to some incredibly deft work on the part of Miss Frank in arousing The Divine at such an ungodly hour), the bedraggled twosome arrived at a small airport in the woods just north of Gothenburg.

Miss M took one look at the plane and swooned. She had heard that the Swedes were into suicide, but this was ridiculous. Still, there seemed to be no choice but to board the fragile aircraft. Wrapped to the point of suffocation in multifarious layers of unfamiliar animal skins, and still fighting off the effects of last night's celebrations, Miss M was sullen but obedient as the pilot strapped her into her seat.

"Now, you realize," the pilot said, "there will be some bumping about. Perhaps even some yawing. . . ."

"Yawing?" Miss M yawned in his face. "What's yawing?"

"The unpredictable lurching of the aircraft from side to side," the pilot explained. "Nothing to be alarmed about."

Miss M regarded the pilot with his firm chin, his steel-blue eyes. She surveyed his immaculate blond hair, his strong, broad shoulders. And she was reassured.

And indeed, the flight began pleasantly enough. The lovely Swedish countryside swept by below them in all its fall grandeur: immense stands of dark-green firs, broken hither and thither by orange maples and pale-yellow aspens. And everywhere the lakes, like so many compact mirrors, reflected the afternoon sun. Miss M looked down on the endless stretches of the by-now familiar wilderness and felt the pressures of the tour slide off her back like a fine chinchilla stole. She snuggled back into her seat and closed her eyes.

She wasn't asleep for long. The first hint of trouble was a sharp, definite yaw to the right as the plane flew into a line of mean-looking clouds dripping with rain.

"Just a bit of turbulence," the tall, broad-shouldered pilot shouted to his passengers in the back.

But Miss M's ears, sensitive as a hound's, heard the trace of concern in the pilot's voice. Still, he had such blond hair. Surely nothing could go wrong.

The second sharp lurch, however, was more than a yaw. The plane moved not only sideways, but definitely downwards as well. Miss Frank looked angrily at Miss M and dolefully up to the Lord.

"It's just a bit of turbulence," said Miss M.

"It's the engine," the pilot called back. "I'm afraid we'll have to land."

Miss M looked out the window, her mind racing through every aviation movie she had ever seen. Land? There *was* no place to land. Only more of those endless pine trees and those goddamn maples.

"I'm going to try over there by that farmhouse," the pilot said.

Miss M peered down intently. Not far below, she could make out a small wooden-frame house with a large open field behind it. How pitiful, Miss M. thought, that after blistering my heels so badly on the ladder of success, I should come to my end on this little plot of ground in the middle of nowhere. The headline she would never see danced before her eyes:

SUPERSTAR KILLS PIG IN FATAL PLUNGE

Began Career at Continental Baths

The pilot shouted back orders: "Fasten your seat belts tightly. Remove all sharp or breakable objects from anywhere around you. Bend your heads towards your knees. Wrap your arms around your heads. Above all, relax!"

The plane lurched about more helplessly than ever in the wind and rain. They descended rapidly toward the field below. When they were twenty feet above the ground, the pilot cut the engine completely. The silence was terrifying. But Miss Frank was brave. The pilot was brave and tall and broad-shouldered. Miss M was none of the above. The plane landed in a field of clover as if nothing were wrong.

"We are in Paradise," Miss Frank announced. "Praise the Lord."

"Actually," the pilot said, "we're in Weldmere. About one hundred miles southeast of Stockholm."

"We're up Shit's Creek is where we are," The Divine chimed in with her usual eloquence. "And what, may I ask, do we do now?"

The pilot was about to respond when a loud Hallo! drew everyone's attention outside. Running toward them through the field was a wild-eyed, white-haired man accompanied by two beautiful young women and a gaffer. Waving what appeared to be a megaphone, the man and his companions approached the battered plane.

*I*magine The Divine's surprise when she saw that the man, whom she had taken to be some crazed pig farmer, was in fact the renowned film director Vilmos Angst. Imagine his surprise when he saw it was The Divine who had fallen out of the sky into the middle of his location. Miss M threw off her restraining straps, dashed out of the plane and embraced the genius madly.

Miss Frank, who had never heard of Vilmos Angst, thought the forced landing had driven Miss M loony and shouted for her to get back into the plane and behave like a lady.

But Miss M was beyond hearing, so delirious was she over this opportunity to meet, albeit under peculiar circumstances, the world-famous genius of cinematic art. Who knew where this could lead?

It led, almost immediately, to a large barn located near the farmhouse Miss M had seen from the air. There Mr. Angst was filming his newest epic in total secrecy.

The barn's interior had been renovated to resemble a medieval sauna, complete with giant crucifix and plenty of fir boughs.

"This film, which I shall call *Thighs and Whispers*," Angst explained, "represents a departure for me. It will be a comedy of manners, in which pain and guilt and man's inborn need for humiliation and despair will play only a minor part."

"That's too bad," Miss Frank interrupted.

"Actually, the plot is quite simple, since, along with other things, I am eschewing the convolutions of my past work: A young nun, who has run away from a sadistic Mother Superior and a string of petty thefts from the convent treasury, arrives in the middle of the night at the home of a rich and titled dwarf. She begs sanctuary. The dwarf, who has been a recluse for most of his life, preferring the company of his books and pet baboon to the hurly-burly of the world at large, believes the nun to be a messenger, the instrument of God, sent to him for his salvation, and so agrees to provide the exhausted and kleptomaniacal nun with shelter, hoping to learn, during the night, of the mysteries of her mission. Although somewhat dismayed by the sight of the clearly vicious baboon, not to mention the somber intensity of the dwarf, the nun thanks him for his hospitality and comes into the castle, closing the door on the night and the world outside.

"There, you see? The situation is rife with comic possibility, is it not?"

"It is genius. Sheer genius," Miss M replied, tuned-in as ever.

"And you," Angst continued, "you must be in it. Now that you are here, for you not to be part of my work would be unthinkable."

"But what would I do?" Miss M asked. "You seem to have developed a two-character plot. Three if you count the baboon."

"You shall be Urtha, Goddess of Fire!" he cried. "Urtha, who figures so largely in the dwarf's dreams. I did tell you the dwarf has dreams, did I not?"

"No, I don't think you did," Miss M replied.

"Well, then, let me explain. . . ."

But at that very moment, the pilot returned dripping with grease and announced that the engine was repaired and the weather fine. They would have to leave immediately if Miss M was to get to Stockholm for her performance.

"But you can't leave now!" Angst cried. "Now that I have seen you, no one could possibly play Urtha for me but you, darling, you! If you go, I shall have to cut her out of the film altogether. And then what shall I do? No dreams; no movie."

"Well then," Miss M replied, "let the baboon dream. Of *his* goddesses."

"Why . . . why, that's brilliant!" the world-famous genius exclaimed. "Brilliant! Frieda! Bring me the script!"

As Miss M left the barn, Vilmos Angst was scribbling furiously in the tattered pages of his notebook. "The *baboon* must dream," he cried again and again. "The *baboon!*"

––––––––––

"What was *that* all about?" Miss Frank asked as the two women plodded across the meadow to the waiting plane.

"That is the climax of two thousand years of Western civilization," Miss M answered proudly.

"That's our punishment, if you ask me" was all Miss Frank said.

And perhaps Miss Frank was right. As we shall see in Part Two of *The Continuing Saga of The Divine Miss M.* ––◗•••

*L*et us talk for a moment about chauffeurs. When you're out on tour, wherever you may be, the native with whom you come in contact most is the man whose job it is to drive you to and from the airport, hotel, hall and restaurants, the man who also tends to be your guide on sight-seeing junkets and shopping sprees. In other words, your chauffeur.

For a chauffeur, enthusiasm, patience and a keen sense of the ridiculous are very important, especially when driving folks who are longing to see the sights but haven't the vaguest notion what the sights are, or why, indeed, they are sights at all. Couple this ignorance with the fact that such grimly uninformed travelers are invariably in a hurry, and you can readily understand why the life expectancy of a chauffeur, especially in the non-English-speaking countries, is *much* shorter than that of almost any other worker involved in a service industry. In fact, one of my chauffeurs explained to me that many of the stone markers one sees along the highway are not kilometer signposts, as one might think, but rather dainty gravestones marking the spot where various chauffeurs have dropped by the wayside. I myself saw such a stone engraved: *"HERE LIES LARS SCHAV. HE DROVE JOEY HEATHERTON. R.I.P."*

My driver in England was named Bert, and he was quite extraordinary. Overweight, but underwhelmed by anyone of any station. The only thing Bert ever really tipped his hat to was a good dirty joke. Or a bad one. In fact, Bert *preferred* the bad ones, which made me like him even more. To show you what I mean, here's Bert's all-time favorite:

BERT'S FAVORITE JOKE

Have you heard the one about the fat little boy who was so dumb he thought "sex" was the past tense of "six"? He finally earned his dunce cap when a teacher who thought he was getting too plump asked him how many slices of bread he ate each day.

"Oh," the lad replied, "I have sex in the morning, and I have sex at night. Sometimes I even have sex for luncheon."

Well, word got around that the little chap did not want to be dumb anymore, so a very enterprising schoolmate picked up some rabbit droppings and put them in a jar. He went to see the dunce and said, "You want to be smart, heh?"

The dumbo nodded.

"Tell you what," the rascal said, "I have some smart pills here. You can have 'em for a quid."

Well, the little boy was ecstatic. He paid the chap a quid and started to chomp on the pills. "Holy mackerel," he cried, "these taste like shit!"

"You see?" the other replied. "You're getting smarter already."

How could I help but be charmed by a man who told with the greatest enthusiasm jokes even older and more gruesome than mine?

Another chauffeur I will never forget was Josef, my driver in Copenhagen. In his late forties and about five feet tall, he was a pint-sized version of a classic Viking god.

One day on a sight-seeing drive around Copenhagen's famous harbor, Josef stopped in front of an old and graceful yacht that was tied up in the notorious Sailors' Quarter.

"She's beautiful, no?" Josef smiled at the boat like an old lover.

"Definitely, beautiful," I said, "and what a wonderful name it has—*Englen med Sorte Vinger*. What does it mean?"

"*The Angel with Black Wings*," Josef answered.

"Oh," I said, "that's a sort of scary name for a boat, don't you think?"

"Not really," he said, turning around in the front seat and

gazing at me with his calm blue eyes. "It's from an old Danish fairy tale about a baby mouse who steals up into the attic to nibble on some cheese he's swiped from the family larder. Tired and full, he's just about to fall asleep when a bat flies in the window, directly over his head. In a flash, the little mouse is up and racing downstairs to his mother. 'Oh, Mama, Mama,' he cries, his heart beating with excitement, 'guess what I just saw!' 'What, dear?' Mama Mouse asks her little baby. 'Something wonderful,' the little mouse exclaims. 'An angel with black wings!'

"Oh," Josef said, "if only *we* could dream up such fanciful interpretations for our visions in the night! I've always loved that little mouse for seeing an ordinary bat as something so mystically beautiful. That's why I named the boat after his story."

"*You* named the boat?" I asked, surprised.

"Well, I did. Yes. The boat is part mine, you see. Originally it was my father's. Now it belongs to the whole family. Would you like to see it?"

Of course I wanted to see it and from its gleaming wood hull to its polished mahogany interiors, *Englen med Sorte Vinger* was quite the loveliest vessel I had ever been on. Sensing my enthusiasm, Josef asked me if I would like to see a part of the boat he didn't usually show to anyone. When I said yes, he opened a small hatch in the middle of the cabin floor that I hadn't noticed before and climbed down a rickety ladder, motioning for me to follow.

I descended into a small space so dark I could barely see and for one fleeting instant wondered if it was only his boat Josef wanted to show me. But as my eyes became accustomed to the half-light, I saw that the walls of this lower cabin were covered with yellow cloth Stars of David. Suddenly the whole day changed.

"During the War," Josef said, "we ferried Jews to Sweden. Every star is a Jew we saved. Or tried to save. There are maybe forty or fifty stars there, and we never got caught. My father was the town's greatest fisherman and a master at masquerade. He would give the German guards his freshest eels, sometimes even a lobster if we had been lucky enough to haul one in. He gave the Germans the best of his catch, and they never caught on to what he was doing. Well, towards the end of the War they did, but by then they didn't care. They just wanted to go home, like everybody else."

I was flabbergasted. And moved. Then upset to think how little of what we Americans hear or are taught we really absorb, how little of it really penetrates the heart. For of course I had heard about the Danish underground and the escape route across water to Sweden, but until the moment I stood in that dark, cramped cabin with Josef it was never real to me, more like a movie I had seen once long ago, then promptly forgot.

I tried to remember where I had first heard about Denmark and the Yellow Stars. Probably in school. Then I remembered I had learned almost nothing in school. In world history I had only gotten as far as Ponce de Leon. (Oh, Ponce! Ponce! The most sensitive and sensible of all the explorers.) Suddenly I wanted to make up for that lack; I wanted to know all I could about World War II, World War I—everything. I brooded. Finally, in utter humiliation and under cover of darkness, I forced myself to buy and read a twelve-pound volume titled *Wars*.

I realize twelve pounds is not quite enough weight to constitute truly far-reaching research, but I found out what I needed to know: that what we live through every day is a continuation of the Battle of Jericho, and that there is a kind of Sleazy Nationalism which breeds within the breast of the citizen confusion, dissatisfaction and a burning desire to get what his neighbor's got or what he *thinks* he's got or has been *told* he's got. In other words, paranoia, avarice, acquisitiveness, glory seeking (which is really only vanity, after all) and, yes, folks, let us be brave, BOREDOM on a scale so vast as to be incomprehensible are the causes of war and always have been.

It was a heavy book, in every way. However, it wasn't the reading I minded, it was the carrying that wore me out. I stuffed *Wars* into the satchel I always carry in my right hand. After two weeks of lugging it from country to country, my right arm and breast swelled to such gigantic proportions that I was forced to cut off my sleeves and go without a bra. Not a good idea for a hefty young woman even in her own homeland, (not to mention on foreign soil, where bleached-blond women are traditionally treated as Magdalenes, and a bleached blonde with black roots, a swollen breast over her shoulder, and no baby in sight is likely to be treated even worse). I finally gave the book to Miss Frank to carry and managed to hide my deformity by wearing my Karl Lagerfeld camel's-hair coat backwards until the offending members returned to their former, nonengorged state.

I was relieved when I finished it and neither Miss Frank nor I had to carry the goddamned book around anymore. In the end we managed to put *Wars* to pretty good use, though. What was not biodegradable can probably still be found floating among the debris of the great sewage systems of the world where toilet paper is just a hope of the future, although chauffeurs, of course, are not.

The most amazing thing happened to me while I was in Copenhagen. I wanted very much to lay my eyes on the Little Mermaid, who had, after all, been my inspiration for Dolores.

The Danes had gone simply wild over Dolores, sensing that the nutty fruitcake in the wheelchair was, in some crazy way, a tribute to their national heroine. It seemed only fitting that I pay the little statue a visit.

The day we left on the short drive to the harbor where she sits, gazing out toward Sweden, was gray and gloomy. On the horizon, thunderheads were gathering, threatening rain. Or worse. The weather was so bad, in fact, that Josef suggested we turn back and see the lady some other day.

But there *was* no other day for me. On the morrow I would be leaving for Paris and the French Experience, so it was, quite literally, now or never.

"But she is so much more lovely in the sunlight," Josef insisted. "Perhaps it is better that you don't see her at all than see her in so unbecoming a light."

"That's all right," I told him. "I know all about unbecoming light."

So on we drove through the gray-green town. Large drops of rain splattered like broken eggs on the windshield. The sky grew darker and darker as chilly gusts of wind nearly shook the car off the road. I thought of *The Little Match Girl* and *The Red Shoes* and shivering Jews crossing in the night to the haven of Sweden, just a few miles across the Öresund.

By the time we reached the small green slope which leads down to the water's edge where the Little Mermaid sits so patiently, loud claps of thunder split the black and swirling air.

"We must park here and walk a bit," Josef said. "Are you sure you want to go?"

"I must," I told him, gathering up the collar of the same brown coat I had worn backwards and forwards throughout all of Europe.

We climbed out of the car and walked towards the water, our heads bowed against the stinging wind and rain.

"Tell me when we get there," I shouted at Josef above the breaking thunder.

"All right," he said. And then, in a moment, "We're there."

I stopped walking and lifted my head. Not more than ten feet from where I stood was the Little Mermaid. I hope she's not angry with me, I mumbled, thinking of that loudmouthed wretch Dolores.

Just then a huge, mean-looking cloud blew in off the sea and hung over the shoreline, enclosing the Little Mermaid and me in a misty envelope of silence and chill. All around the base of the statue green-black waters began to swirl and foam. It became so dark I thought someone had put out the sun. It was eerie.

I was just about to turn and run back to the car when a clap of thunder exploded directly overhead, and at the very same instant, a bolt of lightning as bright and fierce as anything I've ever seen struck the defenseless statue right on the noggin. For one incredible, breathtaking moment, the Little Mermaid glowed pure gold.

I turned to Josef, my mouth hanging down to the ground, but in his perfect politeness he had already returned to the car so that the Little Mermaid and I might be alone for a while. He had missed the entire event. In all the world, I was the only one who had seen it.

I suppose there will be other moments in my life as awesome and mysterious, but none, I think, more moving. For there in that little country of cottage cheese and courage, I became a child again, and for the first time since I was six, I felt something we all should feel at least once a year but hardly ever do: the thrilling rush of insignificance.

"Hath not a mermaid eyes?
Hath she not ears?"

We were traveling at quite a clip down one of those twisting coastal roads that seemed to fill up every other frame of the tackier Nouvelle Vague films of the early sixties. Memories of innumerable Fiats plunging into the sea kept crowding out of my brain the beauty that lay before me. It was a gorgeous, sunny day. The kind of day when the English Channel is the color it ought to be, not the dismal gray it usually is. The leaves were falling, the birds were singing and oh, boy, did I have gas!

Not from anything I had eaten, mind you, but from acute aggravation. And who was the cause of my aggravation? You guessed it: Dolores.

I hated to admit it, even to myself, but ever since her triumph in London and on the Continent, Dolores had been getting cockier and cockier. That pushy piece of tail was capable of doing anything. And did.

Everyone was a victim of Dolores' incredible self-indulgence.

One night she couldn't get her poi balls to work. So the indefatigable woman stopped and started again. And again. And again. And again. For a good fifteen minutes she stood there, center stage, smashing balls into her eyes, her nose, her lovely set of boom-boom curls. Still she wouldn't give up until her mastery was proved—as if by then anyone cared. By the time she quit, the drummer's hands were raw and bloody. The conga player needed oxygen. The trumpet player's lips had fallen off.

I had created a monster: of that there was no doubt. Then, in Fontainebleau, where we were spending the night after a long but picturesque detour to savor the joys of Brittany's cuisine, it happened. Without a word of warning, Dolores flew the coop. Took off. On her own. Just like that. It must have been quite a sight: Dolores, dragging her tail behind her, starfish bra bouncing proudly, walking right out of the theater and into the world outside. And she had the gall to take my three yentas with her.

Naturally, she headed for the beach, which is where they finally found her, brazenly drying her scales in the sun like so many pounds of dead fish.

"I will no longer be confined to the stage!" she shouted as they tried to pry her off a rock and into the waiting van. "Why should I be? Hath not a mermaid eyes? Hath she not ears? If you prick me, doth I not bleed?"

Oh, Dolores, I thought. Give it a rest.

Still, it really was quite something. My Ladies had never dared to go out on the street before. I don't think they were brave enough. Or I wasn't brave enough to let them. Now, strange as it was, there was something about what Dolores did that very much appealed to me. For when I really came to think of it, why were my Ladies chained to the stage? Why shouldn't they get to go out now and then?

"I had created a monster."

Why? Why? Why does that woman treat me so shabbily? Where does she come off trying to tell me what to do on stage! I don't tell *her* what to do. How could anyone tell her anything? She thinks she's so high falutin' with her phony blond hair and her high-heeled shoes (which she *says* are Charles Jourdan. Hah!) and her stupid name in lights. So what! is what I say. So *what!* That doesn't give her the right to accuse me of behaving recklessly. The nerve to tell me I'm making too much out of my balls! My audience *wants* to see me triumph! *Needs* to see me triumph! Doesn't she understand what a symbol I am? My victory is *their* victory! I give them hope! I show them what courage *means!* She's jealous, that's all. She likes to think she's the only one who has ever tasted success, who's ever done anything worthwhile. Hah! Who will ever forget *my* work in *Porgy and Bass* or *Finny Girl* or the ever-popular *Goldilox?* Not to mention my autobiography—*Fear of Frying!* Even now I am at work on my next offering: *Household Hints from the Toast of Chicago.* Of course with all the ruckus around here I've only gotten two chapters done—*How to Get Rid of Silverfish* and the very important *How to Beat Copper into Submission.* Let her match that! She wants to compete. I'll give her compete. Eat or be eaten, I always say. That's what this whole world's about. Well, that and Art, of course. Which is something else about which she knows nothing. Especially *my* Art. I am a serious artiste. My work has shape and form. It is not, I repeat *not,* a repellent monument to megalomania, as is the work of some we know. My Revues, my Medleys *are* my Message. But does that wretched vat of moral decay ever think about the thought and care that go into what I do? Let me see *her* sing "The Moon of Manakoora" in a wheelchair and make it work! But I don't get appreciation. I don't get a Thank you. I get ridiculed. And laughed at. That's what I get. Well she won't have Dolores to kick around much longer, I can tell you. She's nothing but an overbleached, overboobed fraud. And I intend to tell her so . . . tomorrow.

"Well she won't have Dolores to kick around much longer . . ."

"Miss Frank! Miss Frank!" I shouted, looking out my bathroom window for the first time and feeling a thrill run through my body, "Guess where we are!"

"Paris, dear," the impossible woman replied as she struggled to clean up a particularly vivid room-service mess left over from the night before. "We've been here for two days."

"Don't be snide," I said. "I meant we're right next door to Les Galeries."

"Oh, how nice for you, dear." Miss Frank was unimpressed. "Why don't you get dressed and go look at some paintings?"

"Les Galeries, darling, is a *department* store. The biggest in Europe."

"Really?" said Miss Frank, her eyes lighting up a bit. "Do you think they have panty hose?"

Poor Miss Frank: hers was an endless quest for panty hose to replace the ones I was destroying at the rate of two or three pairs a night. "Oh, yes, I'm sure they do. Shall we go?"

It took us exactly three minutes to be dressed and out the door. I was especially excited not so much by the thought of purchasing underwear as by the thought that I had finally found a place in Paris where I could buy one of those beautiful French baskets for the back of my brother Daniel's bike. Of course, I had seen many fancy shops on the Rue de Rivoli where I could have bought one, but I was, if the truth be known, scared to death to go in them. Only two groups of people intimidate me absolutely: salespeople and the French. So imagine my terror of having to face a French salesperson! I would be mortified—unable to remember even my name, let alone what I wanted to buy. Once, on a previous trip to Paris, I had gone into a shop by the Louvre to buy one of those wonderful plastic replicas of the *Venus de Milo*. But as soon as I stepped foot in the store all I could think about was whether I had brushed my teeth, and if I had half as much class as the counter display. When the perfectly coiffed saleswoman, dripping with pearls and pretension, turned and asked if she could *"vous aider,"* I fled.

But a department store! That I was sure I could handle. After all, I had been to Bergdorf's and triumphed. Certainly I could deal with Les Galeries, which would be, with all its French signs stripped away, nothing but a glorified K-Mart. As soon as we arrived, I sent Miss Frank off to Lingerie and strode confidently by myself into the basket department.

Oh, what a heavy sigh of relief I breathed when I saw that the salesman in Baskets wasn't wearing a single piece of gold anywhere on his body and was definitely *prêt-à-porter*. There's nothing he can do to me, I thought. I can stay on top of this. Then, taking a moment to form the sentence in my mind, I spoke.

"Bonjour, monsieur," I said proudly. *"Avez-vous un paquet pour les bicyclettes?"*

"Excusez-moi," the salesman replied, "but could you speak a little slower? I don't speak English too well."

"But I was speaking in *French*," I said, my bubble of confidence beginning to burst.

"Alors. Je regrette. Encore, s'il vous plaît."

I began all over, this time just a little slower to make sure of my pronunciation. *"Bonjour, monsieur, Avez-vous un paquet pour les bicyclettes?"*

"Excusez-moi," the salesman said again, exasperation creeping into his voice, "but now what language are you speaking?"

"I'm speaking *French!*"

"I'm sorry, but what you were speaking was definitely not French. Perhaps it was some other language you *think* of as French."

"It was French! Perhaps you weren't listening."

> *"Only two groups of people intimidate me absolutely: salespeople and the French."*

"I listened. All day long I listen to people who say they are speaking French, but unless they *are* French, they aren't."

"What you mean is they're not speaking perfect French."

"Anything not perfect is not French. And now shall we proceed? In *English*."

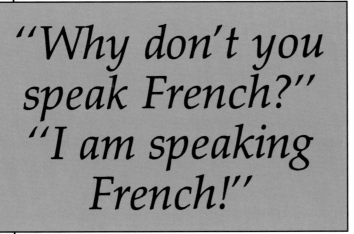

"Why don't you speak French?" "I am speaking French!"

I couldn't believe it. Only in the store two minutes and already I was feeling inadequate and upset. Nevertheless, I did want one of those baskets, so I decided to go on. Things could only get better.

"I would like a basket for a bicycle. Nothing too big." I hoped that was a fairly neutral statement.

The salesman held up a lovely dark cane basket for me to inspect. "Perhaps something like this?"

"Oh, that would be perfect," I said, "but would it fit on a boy's bike?"

"*Ah, mon Dieu!* Boys' bikes! Girls' bikes! We have no such things here," he almost shouted. "Only in America do bicycles have gender. It's just another part of your obsession with sex!"

"Oh, really?" I said, incredulous that we were going at it again. "The French ain't exactly slouches in that area."

"Ah, but for us sex has always had its time and place. Love-making is an art and, like a great painting, should have a frame around it. You have lost that notion in America. It spills over into everything."

Well, I couldn't disagree too vehemently with *that*.

"You know," the salesman continued as if talking to a child, "In France we always make love. We never have sex. We can't. We haven't got a word for it. And besides, how can you *have* sex? Perhaps you can *make* sex or even *do* sex, but *have* sex? It's very strange."

"Well," I replied, "just think of it like you have a meal or have a laugh."

"I'd rather not," he said. "And now to get back to the baskets."

I was wondering if we ever could, when suddenly Miss Frank emerged from Lingerie, loaded down with what seemed to be hundreds of packages of red and black panty hose. "Oh," she said as she approached, tottering under her load, "this store is wonderful. They have everything."

"But how did you get them to actually sell you anything? What did you say?"

"Say? Who said anything? I pointed, like I always do. Now hurry up; we're late."

"But I didn't buy the basket yet!" I whined.

"You'll have to do it tomorrow. Come on." And so saying, she threw half her load into my arms and began to walk towards the exit.

I looked back over my shoulder at the salesman, who was still holding up the basket and, for the first time, smiling. At first I thought it was a smile of triumph. But then I wasn't sure. There seemed to be something warmer. Or maybe it was just my imagination.

Of course, I never got back to Les Galeries, but when three months later I returned to Los Angeles, a package was waiting for me. It was from Les Galeries, and stuck on top was a little envelope addressed to Miss Midler. I opened up the envelope and found inside a small black-and-white snapshot of the salesman I had encountered there. On the back a little note was scribbled:

Dear Miss Midler,
    We French are an odd lot. And, I know, often disliked. But lest you mistake, as many do, our love for intellectual debate with cold-hearted arrogance, I am taking the liberty of sending you this.

                                            Yours truly,
                                            Jean-Michel

Astonished, I opened the package and there it was: the dark cane basket. And on the bottom of the basket lay a little card in the same handwriting as the note. *For Boys' Bikes Only*, it said. And I know Jean-Michel meant it nice.

Lafayette, we are here!

Ou est le docteur? Le gendarme? Je désire à téléphoner à mon consulat. Ma chambre est trop petite; trop grande. Avez-vous une chambre à deux lits? J'ai perdu ma valise. . . . *Ooh! Excusez-moi, but I only got to Page Two in my phrase book.*

Ah, but it is wonderful to dig our spikes into the beloved soil of La Belle France. Truly, mesdames et messieurs—les *tits, c'est moi! And Paris! Paris! City of Light. City of the tough customer. City of the First Class Subway Token. What a thrill to* épanger *these cobblestones. The moment I got off the plane I knew we belonged here.*

Check the demoiselles à ma gauche. *And I do mean* gauche. *Look at these girls. Talk about Gaul. You see, it really is divided into three parts. Ladies and Gentlemen, a hearty Parisian welcome to three items I picked up on discount at the Common Market—Les Harlettes Formidables! Show them Paris when it sizzles, girls! Aw righty, girls. Enough sizzling. Strike a Gallic pose. (HARLETTES DO.) Not garlic—Gallic. Oh, my, c'est* difficile de trouver des domestiques, n'est-ce pas? Mais ooh, là là! *We are thrilled and delighted to be here in the town where good taste was born. And— judging from the front row—died not moments ago. Really, my dears, you* are the Poor People of Paris. *And this place—the Théâtre Palais. It's so . . . French. Honey, we have played some toilets in our time. This isn't exactly a toilet. It's more unto a bidet. . . . However, I have found in my travels that just as it is not so much the salad as the chef, it is not so much the* théâtre *as the show. Ladies and gentlemen, we offer you this evening Service Compris! Yes, we are going to do it all for you tonight. And to begin, a touching little tune I'm sure you all remember . . . "La Vie en Rose."* **Not** *to be confused with* La Viande Rosé, or The Red Meat . . . *an early but extraordinary film by Godard which subtly limns the superiority of Communist cows over Fascist pigs. Ah, well . . . as Napoleon said while scuttling back from Moscow—"The cheese stands alone,* n'est-ce pas?" *Or words to that effect. It loses in the translation. Much as I myself am losing even as we speak. . . .*

MESDAMES ET MESSIEURS, JE VOUS PRÉSENTE

· MADAME SOPHIE ·

I will never forget it! I was in the woods last night with my boyfriend Ernie and he said to me, "Soph! These woods sure are dark. I sure wish I had a flashlight." I said to him, "So do I, Ernie. You've been munching grass for the last ten minutes!"

I will never forget it! It was on the occasion of Ernie's eightieth birthday. He rang me up and said, "Soph! Soph! I just married me a twenty-year-old girl. What do you think of that?" I said to him, "Ernie, when I am eighty I shall marry me a twenty-year-old boy. And let me tell you something, Ernie: twenty goes into eighty a helluva lot more than eighty goes into twenty!"

Oh, I will never forget it! It was on the occasion of my eightieth birthday. My boyfriend Ernie bought for me a tombstone, and on that tombstone he had inscribed: HERE LIES SOPH. COLD AS USUAL. Not being one to take that kind of thing lying down, I went out and bought Ernie a tombstone, and on that tombstone I had inscribed: HERE LIES ERNIE—STIFF AT LAST!

You know, I will never forget it! I was in bed last night with my boyfriend Ernie and he said to me, "Soph, you got no tits and a tight box." I said to him, "Ernie.

Memo to Miss Frank:

To avert the embarrassment of last night's debacle which, as you know, could

Letter No. 1 (30 copies)

Mayor's Office
City of _____

The Honorable Mr. _____, Mayor of _____:
Dear (First name; use diminutive)

    I was overwhelmed with your floral tributes, and terribly flattered by your beautifully worded wishes of goodwill. Unfortunately, I'm afraid time does not permit us any kind of rendezvous, even the kind you so colorfully described in your note. What a bounteous and vivid imagination you possess.

    In my long and varied career in this business we call show, it has been my pleasure to receive more than a few temptingly scripted notes of this type—curiously enough, the great majority of them from mayors. While those other two "M" girls—Liza and Shirley—seem to specialize in heads of state, I find myself sitting on the knees of the city fathers. Metaphorically, to be sure. Those girls' liaisons are mostly ministerial. Mine are mainly municipal. My run of political suitors tends to be not so much urbane . . . as urban. Ah, well, such is the luck of the toss. Metaphorically, to be sure.

    I must, however, regretfully decline your tempting entreaties. Someday you may thank me for this. I will alert you as to when.

    In any event, allow me to thank you once again for thinking of me and to tell you how sorry I am that my busy schedule does not afford the time for you to come to my hotel and bury your nose in my armpit.

Cordially,

Bette Midler

very well happen again, may I suggest you xerox the following two letters?

Letter No. 2 (2000 copies)

To the Editor, name of newspaper or magazine

Dear Sir:

Of all the outrageous, disreputable lies that you have printed about me in the past, this last pronouncement of yours (Volume ____ Issue ____) is the most outlandish yet and cannot, and will not, go unchallenged! How could you stoop so low as to imply that there is some sordid liaison between myself and Mayor (fill in appropriate name). I have no liaisons, sordid or otherwise; the entire concept is simply too French for my taste, for despite your unending efforts to paint me as a wanton, sex-crazed floozy, I am at heart a simple woman committed to the simple virtues of fidelity and discretion. Why will no one believe me? Why will no one see past my cleavage to the pure heart that beats below? Am I destined always to be everybody's favorite libertine when Ovaltine is really where I'm at? Have a heart, fellas. Give the old Diva a break. Everywhere I go people keep winking at me. And why? Because of the kind of stories you keep printing over and over, week after week. I am upset. The Mayor is upset. We won't even speak of the City Council.

Gentlemen, there is a great and compelling beauty in truth. Trust it. Use it. Or I swear to God I will sue you for every _____ (fill in local currency) you are worth.

Trembling on the brink of a major lawsuit, I remain,

Yours truly,

Bette Midler

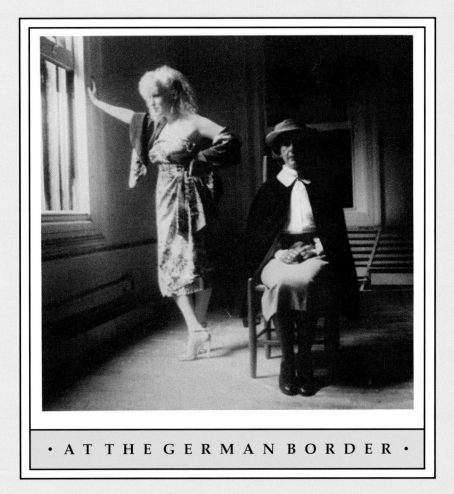

· AT THE GERMAN BORDER ·

" . . . what's the matter? What's wrong? Where are you taking me? Why am I in Immigration? I do not want to immigrate. This <u>must</u> be a mistake. Why do you keep staring at my passport like that? So I'm not a redhead anymore. Didn't you ever hear of peroxide and lemon juice? What's wrong? What's the matter? Where are you taking me? . . ."

FRANKFURT, GERMANY

While I was in Germany, I thought it would be best not to think of certain things, but I had no choice. As part of my show I had been singing the following little ditty:

Hitler had only one big ball.

Goering had two, but they were small.

Himmler had something sim'lar,

But Goebbels

Had no balls

At all!

Well! What was I to do? Leave it in? Take it out? I thought about it and thought about it. Would my leaving it in be considered a hostile gesture? *Was* it a hostile gesture? Did I *feel* hostile? Or would the fact that I felt free to sing it in Germany be taken as a sign that I believed the "new" Germans could deal with it because they weren't responsible? That bygones were bygones? Then again, did I really believe that bygones *should* be bygones? I didn't know what to do.

I talked about it with a few Germans I came in contact with who could speak English. They all seemed to feel that it would be best *not* to sing it. The audience was coming to have a good time. Why bring up a bad dream?

Well, that seemed reasonable enough to me. I resolved to leave Hitler out of it.

But as fate would have it, as soon as I hit the stage, nervous as a cat and ruled, as always, by some imp of the perverse, the first thing that came out of my mouth was—you guessed it—"Hitler had only one big ball, etc., etc., etc."

No one was more shocked than I. But once I started, what could I do but go on? And once I went on, I went on and on. And not alone. I had the audience sing it with me. First slow. Then at a brisker tempo. Three thousand Germans and one very freaked-out Jewess singing "Hitler Had Only One Big Ball" at the top of their lungs right in the middle of Munich.

I still have no idea how the Germans felt about it. Surprisingly, the reviews never mentioned it, nor did any of the Germans I spoke to after the show. I guess they were just being kind. Which is probably more than I had been in singing it. It was so odd. But then, Germany was odd in many ways.

I'm used to attracting some fairly outrageous crowds—in fact, I pride myself on it—but I have never seen anything as extreme as what I got in Germany.

I think the women were even more amazing than the men. More severe, and certainly much tougher. With platinum-blond ducktail hairdos, long, long squared-off nails and no expression whatsoever. Someone once told me that the bear is the most dangerous animal of all because he never changes his expression. So you never know if he's happy or about to attack. I thought a lot about that in Germany. It's true that in the theater they were very polite. They laughed loudly, applauded warmly. But as soon as the outburst was over, their faces would return to mannequin-like composure. Very Helmut Newton.

The men tended to have a bit more expression, but also a lot more leather. And they came in irons of every variety, from metal-studded chokers to handcuffs. Sitting in my dressing room and listening to the clanking of metal as the audience came in, I thought I was about to perform for a chain-link fence.

I must admit it was a little alarming. Group conformity scares the pants off me because it's so often a prelude to cruelty towards anyone who doesn't want to—or can't—join the Big Parade. I

> *". . . platinum-blond ducktail hairdos, and no expression whatsoever. Very Helmut Newton."*

saw a particularly horrible example of that when I was growing up in Hawaii, and I've never been able to get it out of my mind.

There was a boy in our sophomore class named Angel Wong. Even in Hawaii, where intermarriage is so common, a Chinese–Puerto Rican was an unusual hybrid. Unfortunately, the combination plate that was Angel Wong wasn't exactly the best of both worlds. Angel was about four feet six inches tall and painfully skinny. He had huge black completely crossed eyes and quite an overbite. Furthermore, one leg was slightly shorter than the other, so he walked with a strange little limp that made his head bob up and down like a chicken's. Angel, in other words, *did not come up to standard*, and was, thereby, a perfect target for every joke, practical and verbal, that kids could dream up.

Angel did have one thing going for him though: beautiful hands. And he put those hands to very good use. He was the best bass fiddler our high school ever had.

Unfortunately, the sight of Angel carrying around a bass-fiddle case twice as big as he was proved irresistible to some of my more sadistic classmates.

One day, during a break in orchestra rehearsal, some of the bigger boys, led by Jojo Sagon, a Filipino with a chip on both his shoulders, picked Angel up, threw him into his empty bass-fiddle case, and locked him in. They thought the whole thing terrifically funny. When our teacher, Mrs. Kiyabu, called every-one back and, noticing that Angel was missing, asked where he was, the boys opened the case, to everyone's great amusement.

Yes, the joke was extremely successful. Even Angel smiled a little when he was finally let out of the case, although I remember thinking at the time that it wasn't a smile of amusement exactly. For the rest of the day, Angel didn't say a word to anyone, which just confirmed everyone's feeling that Angel was at heart aloof and unlikable and deserved whatever he got.

Angel didn't go home that afternoon or that night, nor was he anywhere to be found the next morning. His parents, who to-gether could barely speak a word of English, came to the school to find out what had happened, but in a stirring display of school unity no one would tell them the truth.

Finally, about a week later, Angel was found, hanging from a eucalyptus tree about ten miles out of town. On the trunk of the tree, he had tacked up a little sign: I'M TIRED OF BEING THE PUNCH LINE.

I thought a lot about Angel in Germany, where not so long ago *I* wouldn't have come up to standard. In fact, I was thinking about him when Miss Frank came bouncing into my room one morning and threw a little guidebook on my bed.

"Get up!" she said in that tone only mothers usually use. "We're going."

"We are? Where?" I asked, squinting my eyes in the sunlight that was suddenly flooding the room.

"To Salzburg, of course," said Miss Frank as if we had planned it for days. "It's beautiful. And it's in Austria."

So the cagy woman was reading my mind again. I watched as she busily laid out the clothes she decided I should wear. I thought about the punishment she always said was coming. Well, I still didn't know about that. But I knew as long as I had Miss Frank, I surely had my reward.

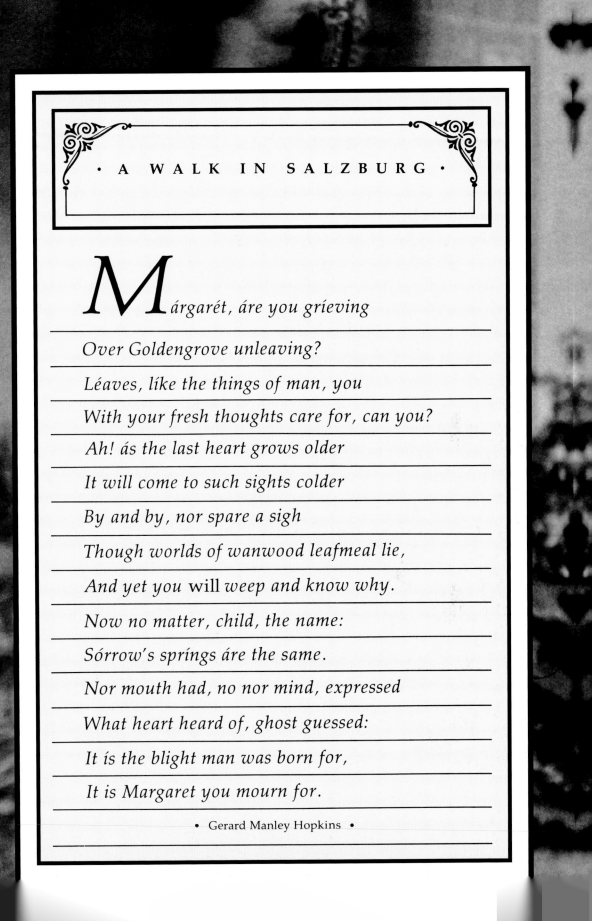

· A WALK IN SALZBURG ·

Márgarét, áre you grieving

Over Goldengrove unleaving?

Léaves, líke the things of man, you

With your fresh thoughts care for, can you?

Ah! ás the last heart grows older

It will come to such sights colder

By and by, nor spare a sigh

Though worlds of wanwood leafmeal lie,

And yet you will weep and know why.

Now no matter, child, the name:

Sórrow's spríngs áre the same.

Nor mouth had, no nor mind, expressed

What heart heard of, ghost guessed:

It ís the blight man was born for,

It is Margaret you mourn for.

· Gerard Manley Hopkins ·

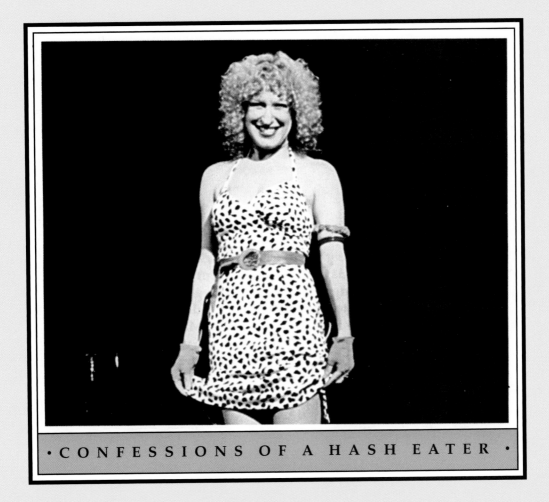

· C O N F E S S I O N S   O F   A   H A S H   E A T E R ·

"I don't take anything. I'm high on life."

I had often heard it said that God created the world, but the Dutch created Holland. Well, at least God rested on the seventh day. The Dutch never do. I don't ever remember seeing a town so on-the-go as Amsterdam. In fact, the Amsterdammers are as industrious when they play as they are when they work. Maybe when you live on land that by natural right ought to be sea, you take everything very seriously, even pleasure. In any case, the Dutch go at their fun with intense determination. And for the weekend of the 16th of October, they had determined that their fun would be me.

The fact was that I was better known in Holland than anywhere else on the Continent, and expectations were running high. There was too much to live up to. I like to whip the crowd up myself rather than have them all whipped up before I even get there. When an audience is that excited, there's no place left to take them. And then what's a poor girl to do? Well, I'll tell you what I did. I ate hash.

Mm, boy, was that a big mistake! For despite any rumors to the contrary, I am, except for an occasional salt pill, essentially drug-free. I used to do a little routine in my act that went like this: First I'd say in a real Scarsdale voice, "Harry! Where does she get all that energy from? She must take something, Harry. What do you think she takes?" Then I'd say, very dramatically, "I don't take anything. I'm high on life." I can hear it in the balcony now!—"Where can I get some?"

It was a dumb little bit, and it was corny. But it was also true. Only once before in my career had I gone onstage stoned, and that was in St. Louis, almost three years before.

On that unforgettable night, I snorted a bit of something the promoter, with only the best intentions, had left for me on my dressing table. It was hardly enough to do any normal person harm, and I felt I was entitled. That tour had been a killer, and I was exhausted. So I snorted it and went onstage.

Four and a half hours later, I was *still* onstage. I sang every song I knew and quite a few I didn't. But of course, I didn't just sing. I expounded at length on such up and entertaining topics as How Do You Think the Soul Feels at the Moment of Violent Death? And the oh-so-cheerful, oh-so-amusing What to Do About the Highway Slush Fund.

At one point during that sterling performance, I left the stage altogether, not to interact more closely with the audience, but to walk out to the candy counter in the lobby, where I bought and consumed an entire quart of buttered popcorn before being returned to my right and proper place.

In every way, the show and I were disaster areas, and I punished myself for it for months afterwards.

So I certainly should have known better in Amsterdam. But, as I said, I was a wreck, and everyone kept telling me how great the hash was and how they ate tons and tons of it and were feeling terrific and how it would relax me and I would be wonderful and funny and full of cosmic energy.

Well, what I was, was nauseous beyond belief. But the nausea took a back seat to the waves of Nameless Terror that came flooding over me with tidal-wave force. I looked out towards the stage

". . . I would be wonderful and funny and full of cosmic energy."

from my dressing room and saw a dark, cavernous abyss where soon I would be led only to be flailed and humiliated by those who had claimed to adore me not ten minutes before. My fears weren't lessened. They were heightened. Not just heightened. Blown out of all proportion.

I tried desperately to talk myself down. I tried to do my vocal runs, my exercises. I tried to remember my name. But I had truly gone to Gouda. And I was terrified.

Miss Frank, of course, knew something was wrong the minute she walked in and saw me sitting inside the wardrobe case sucking my thumb. She offered me some tea, but not much sympathy. She had been with me in St. Louis and heard me swear never to work stoned again.

"How do you feel?" she asked.

"Sick," I said.

"How sick?" she wanted to know.

"Very, very sick," I said.

"Good" was all she said, and then she quickly left the room.

How heartless! I exclaimed to myself, my mind struggling to form even that self-pitying thought. I'm going to find that woman and tell her what I think of her! But I could barely put one foot in front of the other. And curtain time was only minutes away!

When my girls came in for our usual preshow chat, they too saw what pathetic shape I was in. Each of them had some advice: a cold shower, a bowl of borscht, a hit of speed. But I knew I was too far gone for any of that. I didn't know what to do. But, as always, Miss Frank did.

I had no idea where she had gone after she left me so abruptly a few minutes earlier, but now she came back to the dressing room carrying a large book under her arm. As she got closer, I saw that the book was, in fact, my reference tome to all known medical diseases, which hadn't been opened since I bought it. "Here, dear," Miss Frank said, "I want you to see something." "Really, Miss Frank," I said, feeling dizzier by the minute, "I don't want to look at that book now." "Oh, yes, you do," she answered back, shoving before my face a two-page full-color photograph of advanced mytosal phelyngitis, featuring in gruesome detail both rear and frontal views. Shrieking and heaving like the sea, I fled into the bathroom.

When I came back out, I was quite a bit lighter and sober as a nun. Miss Frank was waiting, dog dress in hand. She didn't say a word to me as she zipped me in or even as we walked to the wings, where I waited to make my entrance. But just as the curtain went up and the timpani roll began, she leaned over and kissed me on the cheek.

"Goodness, you looked so sick," she said, and even in the semidarkness I could swear I saw a tear in her eye. "Well, go on, get out there. Before I jab you with this needle."

I gave my light man the cue to go. As the house lights went to black, I could hear the crowd shouting and stamping in anticipation. I looked back over my shoulder for Miss Frank. But she was gone. She knew I didn't need her anymore, and she had work to do. And, her absence told me, I did too.

With a smile to the girls that said, I'm okay, I picked up my mike, straightened my hem, threw out my chest and strode onto the stage.

"Oh, Amsterdam, Amsterdam," I shouted to the crowd. "What a thrill it is to be here. . . ." And to my fondest surprise, I found I really meant it.

· I VANT TO BE ALONE ·

I told a lie in Amsterdam. A big lie.

The entire troupe, myself included, was scheduled to leave on the Tuesday flight to Sydney, where we were to rest our weary bods before beginning three weeks of performances Down Under. But I didn't want to do that. I had other plans in mind.

I told my manager I needed to be alone for a while, that I wanted to stay in Amsterdam and come to Sydney a few days later. He, of course, supportive as always, objected vehemently. He absolutely forbade me to stay alone in Holland.

I reasoned with him as best I could, but I could see it was hopeless. At first I found his protectiveness almost charming, but as he railed on about how he couldn't possibly allow me to do this, or possibly allow me to do that, I began to feel like a prisoner, and rebelled like a child. I told him that if he didn't let me stay in Amsterdam for a few days on my own, I would simply cancel the dates in Australia and go home.

Reluctantly, he gave me my airplane ticket, if not his blessing. "All right," he said, "stay in Amsterdam. See if I care."

"I will stay," I told him, "and I'll be fine. Don't worry."

Only I didn't stay in Amsterdam. I did something I had dreamed about doing for as long as I could remember. And I did it alone. Because I needed to do something brave and daring and maybe even foolish.

I went to India.

". . . I needed to do something brave and daring and maybe even foolish."

My head was swimming with images of rick-shaws and golden tem-ples as we headed down through the clouds to-wards the steaming jungles of Thailand—a one-night layover on my way to Sydney. But nothing, nothing could have prepared me for what I saw.

There was no land anywhere. Only water. At first I thought my eyes were deceiving me, but as we continued to descend through the steel-gray clouds, I could see that my first impression was correct. The entire country was covered by water. It lay over the farms and the towns, the jungles and the roads. In fact, there *were* no roads as far as I could tell, no *land*marks of any kind. I didn't know it then, but I was arriving smack in the middle of the monsoon season. And the monsoons so far had been partic-ularly severe.

During the taxi ride to my hotel (the very same, I was told, where Somerset Maugham wrote several novels and had a few shirts made), through the lushest of landscapes and ten inches of water, I searched for my malaria pills and wondered how I could see it all in just twenty-four hours without a snorkel and a pair of fins. A talk with my taxi driver, who made English sound like a jazz tune, convinced me that the one thing I had to do was take a rice barge upriver into the jungle and see Thai life *au naturel.* But where would I find a rice barge?

It was easy. Tied up to the pier outside my hotel were twenty barges or more. I didn't waste a moment. Using the same bargaining principles that have allowed me in the past to put a show together for $12.98, I hired a barge for the afternoon and a mere pittance. At least, *I* thought it a mere pittance. After all, I got myself a whole barge for the day, and I still had enough money left over to buy a banana.

As I stepped into the boat, clouds of pink and purple raced low overhead and lightning flashed everywhere. Soaked through to the skin, but with my spirits soaring, I made my way up the River of Kings.

This is what I saw:

Enthralled, I looked up at my boatman to see if years and years of rowing up and down these same waters had inured him to the beauties of the place, but from the broad smile on his face he seemed as charmed as I was. He must have felt me staring up at him, because suddenly he turned that broad grin on me and said, "You like?"

"Oh, very much," I answered.

"You smart," he said. Then suddenly the smile under the straw hat disappeared completely. "And you lucky . . . you see it now. . . . Few years . . . all be gone."

"Gone? But why?" I asked, wondering how this way of life that looked so eternal could ever change. "Will the cities take over?"

"No cities . . . war."

"But Thailand is at peace," I said, trying to remember how long it had been since I'd last had time to read a newspaper.

"Peace? Now maybe, but not soon. Look," he said, pointing at a laughing child about to jump off his mother's banana boat into the bustling river. "In all Asia only Thailand never conquered . . . only Thailand always free. Yet all around us, countries un-free. Maybe they don't stay home . . . maybe they come here. Then what you do?"

"Me?"

"You. Miss America. All Thailand watch you leave Vietnam.

Civil war you say, why we there? We say maybe you right, but maybe you just tired. Everything look different when you live next door. Thailand okay now. But soon maybe we must fight to *keep* her free. Tell me, Miss America with your nice blond hair, you ever let your son fight again with mine?

The question, the whole conversation was so disturbing. I hate moral confusion. I like my right and wrong clear-cut, in vivid black and white, but in Thailand I had definitely stumbled into a very gray area.

In the sixties I had been committed to the antiwar movement and done my share of shouting to "Get Out of Southeast Asia Now" and "Bring the Boys Back Home!" Now here I was faced with a people I adored on sight who might soon have to battle for all they held dear. And if Thailand was attacked by her neighbors, would the United States do anything, after Vietnam, to help her? And where would I stand on the question this time?

As I rode back down the River of Kings, the sun was beginning to set on the beautiful world around me. Temple bells were chiming, and monks were everywhere in their saffron-colored robes. Was this world about to pass away forever?

And if it was, I wondered with a sinking feeling, had I, in my own small, unintentional way, contributed to its passing?

· A U S T R A L I A ·

Subcontinent: the end of the earth*
Land area: 198,007,987 sq. miles
Population: 14,000,000
Largest city: Sydney
Smallest city: Sydney
National dish: Pineapple Pizza
National bird: the Fly
Language: derivative of English, as yet unnamed.

* Traditionally the last place to escape nuclear holocaust.

Australia! Land of jumbucks, billy-bongs, mystery meat pies and the wombat. I looked forward to arriving in Australia more than I had ever looked forward to anything—if you don't count getting my ears pierced.

Being on the road in non–English-speaking countries was exhilarating to the point of breakdown, but the burden of speaking even a few words of the native language from the stage each night was beginning to take its toll. I was becoming the Tower of Babel.

"Dank yu vell," I would tell Miss Frank as she hooked me into my no-nonsense bra, and then unable to stop myself, "*C'est difficile de trouver des domestiques, n'est-ce pas? Wenn's etwas gewalt'ger als das Schicksal gibt, so ist's der Mut, der's unerschütterlich trägt.*"

"Of course, dear," Miss Frank would say, patient as ever, "as soon as I'm finished with this corset."

And not only did we have to change our language every day. We had to change our change. Pounds, kronor, French francs, Swiss francs, drachmae, guilders, Marks. I became so confused I stopped using money altogether. I made what few purchases I required by bartering personal items such as long underwear or short exposés on celebrities unlucky enough to have crossed my all-seeing, all-retentive path.

Happily, Miss Frank assured me that all would be well once we hit Australia. Not only did they speak our language there. They even had the sense to call a dollar a dollar. Of course, theirs was worth more than ours, but I was glad to pay extra for the privilege of being able to count my change again. Yes, hopefully, Australia would save us all from that extra thinking we'd had to do in Europe.

And it did. Once we hit that vast continent Down Under, we didn't have to think again. I came to believe, in fact, that it is a *crime* to think in Australia. Or to eat either, for that matter.

There is no food in Australia. Not as we know it. The natives do, of course, on occasion put matter to mouth, but one cannot possibly call what they ingest food.

Still, I felt happier in Australia than almost anywhere else, because life there is so basically relaxed and uncomplicated. The Australians have the best sense of humor of any of the English-speaking nations. I felt young and carefree again. My whole troupe felt the same about the place. In fact, we left a few of the kids from our crew there. In the alcoholic ward of Sydney General—victims of the Australian national pastime.

But I think, more than anything else, I wanted to see Australian wildlife. Like so many others, I'm sure, the unique aspects of Australia's animal population always held me in thrall. How cute they all would be, I thought: cuddly koalas, gentle kangaroos, feisty little penguins. And, it turned out, how deadly!

My first indication of what Australian wildlife was really all about came when I was walking in a field behind one of the beaches in Sydney, and I saw a sign that said:

WARNING: THIS AREA IS INFESTED WITH TAIPANS. *KEEP OUT.*

Taipans? What the hell were they? Was this just another example of the racial snobbery that some said ran just under the hip Australian veneer? Or were taipans some sort of land mines planted by the Japanese?

As it happened, the next night I was introduced to a young man who lived and worked on an animal refuge in the hills just on the outside of town. He told me what taipans were. In fact, he told me a lot. "You may not know it," he said, "but Australia has more poisonous animals than any other place on earth. Not only *more*. The most deadly. The taipans you wanted to know about . . . they're snakes—big, long, ornery snakes that make the cobra look harmless. But of course, we also have the tiger snake and the brown snake and the death adder. Not to mention the sea snakes, which we're beginning to think are responsible for more deaths than we imagined. And other things, too."

"What do you mean, *other* things?" My eyes darted all around.

"Well," he went on, "We've got the funnel spider—*very* deadly! and the blue-ringed octopus—which can kill you in about thirty seconds; and several varieties of conefish and stonefish; but the deadliest of all, the deadliest living thing in the world, in fact, is the sea wasp. We get it up along the northern coast by the thousands."

"The sea wasp!" I exclaimed. "I didn't know bees could live in the ocean."

"It's not a bee," he said, "it's a giant jellyfish—nasty-looking thing, actually. But don't forget, even the adorable little platypus can put you in the hospital for days."

Well, I was in shock! Australia was awash in venom, the land and sea teeming with things to stop your heart or paralyze your lungs. One could be killed instantly. Anywhere.

But brave and feckless as I am, I refused to allow this information to dampen my enjoyment of either the fauna or anything else in Australia. Every dream has a dark side, after all. I simply dealt with any fear I may have felt in the most direct and intelligent way possible. I never left my room again.

The Magic Lady, however, left hers. Ever since that day in Fontainebleau when Dolores decided to go out on her own, I had been waiting, maybe even hoping, for The Magic Lady to do the same. In Melbourne, she finally did. But unlike Dolores, who, shameless hussy that she is, chose to flash her tail not more than fifty yards from hundreds—nay, thousands—of sun worshippers who couldn't help noticing her, The Magic Lady chose to go where there were no people at all. Only animals. Perhaps after four months on the road and thousands of new people to face every night, an animal refuge was a refuge indeed. In any case, when they finally noticed her missing and went to find her and did find her and took her back, The Magic Lady protested vigorously. "You have no time to go hobnobbing with a bunch of marsupials," the stage manager told her, rather peeved at the problems her outing had caused him. "Then you must *make* time!" The Magic Lady snorted. "For me, for you, for everyone."

And now as I sit here, eight thousand miles away from the nearest kangaroo, I wish to hell we had.

On November 20, 1978, almost a week before we were to wind up the tour in Sydney, Miss Frank left to go home to Boston. It wasn't that we had a fight or any some such; how could I ever fight with Miss Frank? It was simply that our time in Australia had been extended, and then extended some more, and Miss Frank had to get home by Thanksgiving. She had promised her family she would be. And Miss Frank never breaks a promise.

Still, as I saw her board the plane, I had to keep myself from shrieking out and ordering her back. Even though the tour still had a week to go, I knew, as I watched Miss Frank wave goodbye and disappear into the plane, that it was over.

I stayed for a moment to see if maybe I could see her little head peering out the window. But it was no use. Lifting up the collar of that same old brown coat which I had by now taken to wearing backwards *and* inside out, I turned and started back to the car.

A week to go, and no Miss Frank!

That, was my punishment for sure.

I felt myself falling apart. But actually, by Melbourne, *everyone* was falling apart. After four months on the go we all had come down with a severe case of Road Fever, a condition marked by alternating periods of intense silliness and overwhelming despair which has the peculiar quality of being both a disease *and* an addiction.

No one talked about it much, but we all knew that the great circle was almost completed. In a week our little show would take its place on that Big Marquee in the Sky. Still, it wasn't just the realization that the tour was almost over which made everyone display that strain of manic gaiety which is, inevitably, a manifestation of underlying sadness and a sense of loss.

It was something more: you can go around the world for the first time only once, and after that, the question is *What do you do for an encore?*

As I watched Miss Frank's plane disappear, I wished we were starting all over again. After all, there were plenty of places we hadn't been to yet—Lapland, for example. I wondered what the Lapps would think of Dolores, or The Magic Lady. Or me.

And the really extraordinary thing was—I wasn't afraid to find out.

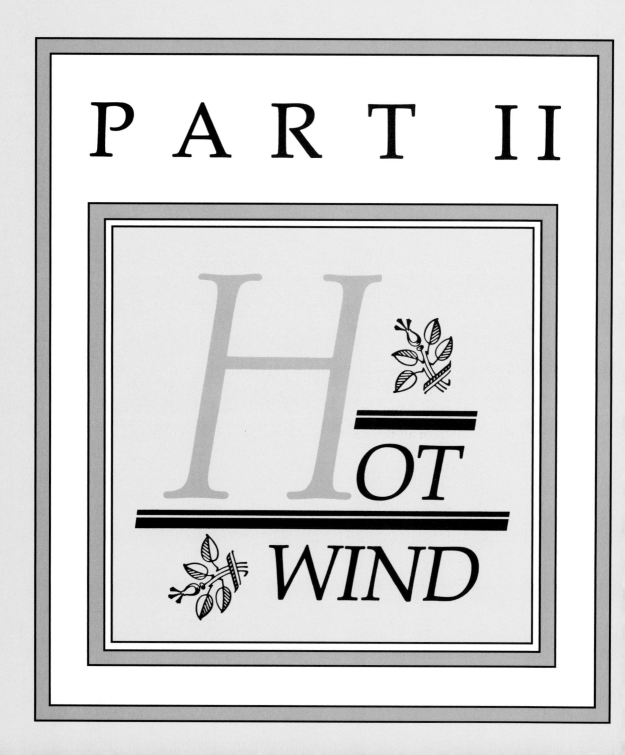

• The Continuing Saga of •
THE DIVINE MISS M

PART II

HoT WIND

When Vilmos Angst first appeared at the door of her suite, wild-eyed and tearful, pleading with Miss M to come back to Sweden and be his Urtha in *Thighs and Whispers*, The Divine was most moved to think that the world's greatest director would come as far as Australia to persuade her to be in his film.

But by his fiftieth appearance, the last one being in her dressing room, which he managed to penetrate by disguising himself as an air-conditioner repairman, Miss M's attitude had changed from one of ego-maniacal delight to sheer annoyance. Where a week ago she had been flattered, now she felt hounded. For Angst refused to take no for an answer. *Thighs and Whispers*, which Angst was certain would be his most important, his most profound film to date, simply could not be made without her. Urtha lay at the very center of the symbolic core of his story, and only *she*, The Divine One herself, could play this most fiery and demented of all the Swedish fish goddesses—the Fish Goddess being, of course, the most revered in all of Norse mythology. Miss M's suggestion that the baboon dream of *his* goddesses, thereby eliminating the need for Urtha, somehow just didn't pan out.

"You see," Angst told her as he popped out from behind a potted palm in the hotel lobby, "the baboon can dream only of *baboon* goddesses. And Urtha must have something more. Something that we can see and understand immediately, something elemental, something to which man has, throughout history, responded to with the greatest passion and commitment—tits."

Well! This little tidbit of character analysis certainly brought Miss M down. Even if Angst's company hadn't been known for paying the lowest salaries in all of cinemadom, The Divine would never have accepted the role. Not now that she knew what she was wanted for. What had she worked all these years for? She was beyond showing her vabooms. Now she wanted to show she could act. And she remained certain there *was* a difference between the two, despite what her manager told her. Still, no matter how firmly she refused him, Angst persisted.

Then, one day while Miss M was walking along a deserted stretch of beach gathering clam shells to send back home as gifts from Down Under, Vilmos Angst, filmmaker and pest, leaped shrieking out of an overhanging gum tree, brandishing in one hand a contract and in the other a .38.

"You must understand," Angst told her, "I don't know yet if it will be you or me. I only know if you don't sign, one of us must die. The death of *Thighs and Whispers* must be avenged. Don't you understand? With this film we, together, could have taken yet another major step out of the . . . the . . . how you say? . . ."

"Stinking hog wallow that we call the field of entertainment?"

"Yes. Very nicely put. So, please. *Var så god.* Sign."

"Mr. Angst, darling," The Divine responded in her most dulcet and reasonable tones, "I just know you wouldn't do anything ungentlemanly —now, would you?"

"Of course not. This contract is eminently fair to both of us."

"I meant with the pistol."

"Oh, that. I'm afraid I would have to. Loyalty to my Muse would demand it."

"Well, then," Miss M said in her most businesslike manner, "you leave me no choice. I'll just go back to my bag and get a pen. Why don't you wait right here? Your feet seem a bit bruised from the fall. You must have been climbing for hours."

"Days," Angst said as he collapsed onto the sand. "Maybe I will wait here. But don't try anything funny. I'll be watching. And aiming."

"I wouldn't think of it," Miss M replied as with the sweetest of smiles she turned and strode purposefully back to where she had left her satchel.

But not to get a pen. She was cleverer than that. Oh, yes, she did have a pen in her bag, but she also happened to have a snorkel and a pair of fins, equipment she had never been without.

Her plan was simple. She would simply jump into her snorkel gear and swim around a small outcropping of rock that separated her from the neighboring cove where her beloved band was gamboling, or what was more likely, gambling, in the sun.

If she could only think of a way to distract Angst for a minute. Happily, Fate was on her side. Shouting to Angst to look up, Miss M pointed to a flock of pelicans heading out to sea to feed on a large school of needlefish. She knew full well that Angst, with his Northern temperament and taste, would be riveted by the sight of a flock of gray birds flying over a gray sea towards an even grayer horizon. Using this distraction to her advantage, Miss M deftly donned her snorkel and fins and dived quietly into the ocean.

Which was *writhing*. Within no more than thirty seconds, Miss M was pulled hundreds of yards out to sea by a raging riptide not even a boat could have bucked. Unfortunately for The Divine, the peculiar nature of snorkeling forced her to keep her head underwater, and since she couldn't tell one patch of kelp from another, she had no idea what the hell was happening. By the time she felt far enough away from Angst to lift up her head and take a look around, she was a good mile offshore, with nothing and no one in sight. Valiantly, Miss M began to swim towards where she guessed, by the position of the sun, the shore ought to be. But since in truth the poor flailing parrot-brain hadn't the foggiest as to where the sun was supposed to be at *any* given hour, she was bravely and briskly heading directly for the South Pole.

On and on she swam, dodging the sea wasps, trying not to give up hope or her stride. But even Divinity has a breaking point, and soon she reached it. Not one more stroke could she force out of her tired, aching body, curse though she might. There was nothing more she could do. Exhausted and resigned, Miss M turned over on her back and closed her eyes, waiting, with a calm she had learned through years of tech rehearsals, for the end. "Death is to the dead as life is to the living," she would often say, although no one ever seemed to know what that meant. Neither did she, actually, but now, *in extremis*, she took comfort, as she had so often in the past, in the magic of things she couldn't understand.

When, at last, the feel of something cold crossing her lips caused her to open her eyes again, Miss M thought she had gone to Glory. In front of her lay a snow-white beach lined with coconut palms bent low, their absinthe leaves caressing a limpid lagoon. Turning her head, she saw a mountain of the most extraordinary grandeur reaching up like a shark's tooth towards the perfect turquoise sky. "Why, this must be . . ."

"Tuamotu," a deep bass voice called out from behind her. At the sound of unexpected company, Miss M whirled around and saw, half-hidden in the crimson hibiscus, a man of such astonishing physical perfection that now Miss M was certain she had hopped the twig.

"I found you lying on the beach," the vision said, his voice as musical as those of the one-and-twenty myna birds perched on his yard-wide shoulders. "My name is Kana. Don't tell me yours. I have made this potion for you from the bark of the tulip tree. Drink it and be strong again beyond illusion."

As the naked Samaritan approached her, holding forth a cup in his huge bronze hands, The Divine could hardly believe her eyes. The whole scene was right out of Central Casting. Too good to be true. Or safe. Maybe her manager was behind it all, orchestrating the entire pageant, laughing into his frangipani leaves. But even if it was for real, anything *this* tempting had better be closely watched. Still, she *was* rather thirsty. And it had been *such* a long swim.

So Miss M took the potion and a number of other things Kana had to offer, including an invitation to enjoy his island for a day or two. After all, she could use the rest, and it was certainly a relief to get away from that moron Angst.

Time on the island, whose exact location Miss M never *could* figure out, went by as languidly and as beautifully as the butterfly fish that drifted lazily in the clear blue lagoon. From sunrise to sunset The Divine lolled about eating and sleeping and slapping away the flies. I could go on like this forever, she thought.

But in actual point of fact, after about three days of sun and surf Miss M began to feel a pull back to what was, for her, real life. "I am a woman of responsibility and commitment," she said to herself one day when the soft, peaceful lap of the waves was particularly annoying. "My life belongs to my public. And besides, if I don't get my feet off of these burning sands, I'll never wear spikes again." She made up her mind to ask Kana to take her back to the mainland—wherever *that* was—as soon as he returned from fishing.

But when Kana finally pulled his outrigger ashore, Miss M saw that he had with him not only his usual string of dead fish, but a fresh newspaper as well. Her heart leaped up at the thought of even this distant contact with civilization, for when all was said and done, The Divine preferred pavement to palm trees and gossip to grouper.

"Here," Kana said, "I got this for you on the Big Island." Miss M ripped the paper right out of his hands. "There's something about you in it."

"Oh, really?" Miss M said, trying to sound blasé but secretly relieved that she was not already forgotten. "Where?"

"On the front page."

The front page! She'd have to remember to give her press agent a bonus. Quickly, Miss M opened the paper, and there, right on the front page just as Kana had said, was a picture of Miss Frank and the girls weeping, and her manager holding up a gold record.

STACKED SINGER SINKS; PRESUMED DEAD

Began Career at Continental Baths

the headline read.

Presumed dead! How perfect! Immediately Miss M changed all her plans. She would not go back to the mainland. Not today. Instead she would wait for the press to actually *pronounce* her dead—they'd been dying to do that for years anyway. Well, let them do it now. Let everyone read that she had joined the Choir Invisible. Maybe then they would all go away and let her be—Angst, her manager, everyone who had tried to control her life for so long. And as for her public, her beloved fans, what could be more dramatic, more thrilling than a Return from the Dead—which, she would carefully arrange for maximum effect?

Miss M threw the newspaper in the air and her arms around Kana. "How about making me one of those drinks of yours?" she said gaily as she tossed Kana's string of limp *poissons* back into the boat. "They can wait. After all, what can a bunch of dead fish do, raise a stink?" And with that godawful pun fouling the innocent air, Miss M and the man she knew only as Kana walked toward the little thatched hut.

Of course, it wasn't until two days later, when the police came and arrested Kana for breaking parole, that Miss M discovered he had been filming the entire idyll in both color and black and white. For pay TV or blackmail, whichever paid more. The Divine was, needless to say, a bit disgruntled, even hurt. Still, she bore no malice. Her feet might be killing her, but after all, the weather had been pleasant, Angst had gone back to his baboon, and Kana *was* gorgeous. Thus with the press clamoring for interviews, her fans falling on their knees in thankfulness for her miraculous resurrection, and her every hair in place, Miss M returned to the Australian mainland, a martyr and a saint, and with her nipples once again firmly to the wind, finished her tour in triumph and in thongs.

AUSTRALIA

. . . Oh, Sydney! Sydney! How you have received me! What love you have shown! I'm so glad this turned out to be a deep, meaningful relationship and not just a one-night stand. God knows, we have had our share of those. Ain't that right, girls? . . . Oh, I tell you, we're just aflutter this evening what with this turnout and this being our last night and all. Of course, we have had a wonderful time flipping and flopping around the world, but on the morrow, my dears, we get to go HOME! I mean I do love you down here—I do—but honey, I'd kill for a Fatburger. . . . But let's face it, kids—once you're out of Sydney, every town is Perth. Let's talk about Perth for a minute. Actually, a minute is about as long as you can talk about Perth. . . . and Melbourne is the kind of town that really makes you consider the question Is there life before death? . . .

You know, I wanted so to leave you with the memory of the good beneath the gaudy, the saint beneath the paint, the pure little soul that lurks beneath this lurid exterior . . . but then again I figured:

Fuck 'em if they can't take a joke!

BETTE MIDLER

ABOUT THE AUTHOR

Bette Midler has been nominated for two Academy Awards and won three
Grammy Awards, four Golden Globes, three Emmy Awards and a Tony
Award. She has sold more than thirty million albums worldwide. She lives in
New York City.